IT 97/8   £13.95

Transforming Schools Through
Collaborative Leadership

Student Outcomes and the Reform of Education

General Editor: Brian J. Caldwell, Professor of Education, Head, Department of Education Policy and Management, University of Melbourne, Australia

Student Outcomes and the Reform of Education is concerned with the reform of public education and its impact on outcomes for students. The reform agenda has gripped the attention of policy-makers, practitioners, researchers and scholars for much of the 1990s, with every indication of more to come with the approach of the new millennium. This series reports research and describes strategies that deal with the outcomes of reform. Without sacrificing a critical perspective the intention is to provide a guide to good practice and strong scholarship within the new arrangements that are likely to provide the framework for public education in the foreseeable future.

1   **School Effectiveness and School-based Management:**
     A mechanism for development
     Yin Cheong Cheng

2   **Transforming Schools Through Collaborative Leadership**
     Helen Telford

Transforming Schools Through Collaborative Leadership

Helen Telford

 The Falmer Press

(A member of the Taylor & Francis Group)
London • Washington, D.C.

UK	Falmer Press, 1 Gunpowder Square, London EC4A 3DE
USA	Falmer Press, Taylor & Francis Inc., 1900 Frost Road, Suite 101, Bristol, PA 19007

First published in 1996

A catalogue record for this book is available from the British Library

Library of Congress Cataloging-in-Publication Data are available on request

ISBN 0 7507 0566 3 cased
ISBN 0 7507 0567 1 paper

Jacket design by Caroline Archer

Typeset in 10/12pt Garamond by
Graphicraft Typesetters Ltd., Hong Kong.

Printed in Great Britain by Biddles Ltd., Guildford and King's Lynn on paper which has a specified pH value on final paper manufacture of not less than 7.5 and is therefore 'acid free'.

Contents

List of Figures and Tables   vii

Abstract   ix

Preface   1

Chapter 1   Leadership: Related Theory and Research   7

Chapter 2   Collaborative Leadership   19

Chapter 3   Research Methodology   28

Chapter 4   The Structural Frame   41

Chapter 5   The Human Resource Frame   58

Chapter 6   The Political Frame   71

Chapter 7   The Symbolic Frame   85

Chapter 8   Further Connections   99

Chapter 9   Issues and Reflections   121

References   137

Appendixes   143

Index   149

List of Figures and Tables

Figure 1: Hypothesized causal map of leadership and school outcomes at the Waratah Primary School 5

Figure 2: Causal network for development of the human rights policy for Wattle Secondary College 6

Figure 3: Elements of collaborative leadership 26

Figure 4: Components of data analysis: Interactive model 31

Table 1: Number of People Interviewed 34

Dedication

This book is dedicated to all those who know what it is to truly collaborate, and in doing so bring shared wisdom, energy and a great sense of perspective to their daily work in places of learning.

Abstract

Since the early 1980s educators in Australia, and around the world, have been faced with continual, radical change in both their schools and the systems that support them. These changes have dominated the workplace. Moreover, the economic and political nature of many of these changes seems to be increasingly taking the reform agenda out of the hands of educators, leaving them with an abiding sense of unease and disorientation. As well, a multiplicity of complex educational demands are being placed at the feet of teachers and administrators. Some schools, such as those in the inner city areas of large cosmopolitan cities are experiencing accelerated changes in the socio-cultural make-up of their student populations, an increasing array of educational expectations and, at the same time, school closures, amalgamations and restructuring at the school and system levels. As these factors converge and impact on those who work, or assist the work, in schools, a shifting context becomes the norm, displacing the once stable and secure basis of educational programs, structures and staffing. Clearly, then, what leaders do to accomplish success in their schools in such unsettling times is of paramount importance. Of particular interest is the contribution of leadership to school improvement in urban schools where perhaps some of the most difficult and intractable conditions prevail. Leaders in these schools are compelled to confront the enigmatic nature of their work head-on if they are to achieve desired outcomes for students, staff and the school as a whole. As a result, successful leaders need to apply peculiar insights and capacities to their workplace, drawing on a sophisticated *modus operandi* which enables them to deal effectively with the problematic school context which faces them on a day-to-day basis. It is with this *modus operandi* that this book is concerned, as it is one which can be practised by not only those who aspire to gain mastery over the crisis conditions that prevail in schools at the present time, but those who also strive to become enlightened leaders of successful schools.

Preface

Context and Intent

In the educational world at the present time there is relentless change at both the school and system level. Schools are in a constant state of reorganization with the dismantling of centralized authorities, including support services and standard operational procedures and processes. Roles and responsibilities of school principals are being revised. Many schools are being closed down as part of government rationalization policy. Others are being amalgamated. Many members of staff are being required to transfer to different schools, whilst others are taking financial packages and early retirement. Moreover, urban schools are confronted with further responsibilities. Students in these schools often come from low socio-economic, non-English speaking backgrounds and have special social welfare and educational needs. Staffing arrangements must serve the specific needs of transient migrant groups, and innovative curriculum provision is a necessity to target the requirements of an urban clientele. Skilful and imaginative leadership, then, is imperative to cope with such a context to bring about success.

This book examines leadership and its links to success in schools, reflecting the view that the role of leaders and the process of leadership are significant contributing factors in the achievement of successful school improvement. Its intent is to establish what it is that leaders *do* as part of their daily work in these schools to achieve success and school improvement, despite the prevailing difficulties. The focus is on the notion of *collaborative leadership*, developed and defined in this book as one which is transformational and encompasses distinctive elements of collaboration. Whilst the study was centred on urban schools in Melbourne, Australia, the insights gained are universal in their application to leadership in schools of all sorts – whether they be large or small, city or rural, elementary or secondary, new or old. For, those of us who work in schools can immediately sense when a school is working well. It sort of buzzes along, at a rattling pace, breathing a life's energy of its own which plays out the hopes, the dreams and the expectations of its inhabitants. Such a school is a place of action, of drama, of politics and of morality. I have been lucky enough to be an inhabitant of just such a workplace and, since that time, it has been an endless source of fascination and intrigue to me to try and determine just how it all comes to be. The purpose of this book is to unravel and share my discoveries, and to attempt to bring a clarity to what has to me always been a murky and confusing scene – effective leadership of a school.

Enlightenment has come from an analysis of the leadership in five inner city schools, both primary and secondary in Melbourne, where for all intents and purposes the odds railed against any likelihood of school success. Many of the students in the schools came from families who were new arrivals to Australia, and from non-English speaking backgrounds. In one of the schools, for example, only ten children in the whole school population had English as their first language. This meant teaching and learning, as well as communication with parents, presented serious difficulties. In addition, many came from low socio-economic circumstances where a social welfare context overlaid the educational one. As well, the predominance of one cultural group was regularly replaced by another within the space of the school year making strategic planning, as far as support staffing was concerned, to a large extent immaterial. Add to this a context of restructuring from a centralized educational authority to self-managing schools, with all of its inherent accompanying complexities, and it was indeed surprising to find that these schools were able to experience such celebrated success. Schools in large cosmopolitan cities around the western world face similar dilemmas, and schools *anywhere* are confronted by what could be described as crisis conditions of information explosion and constant change. To be successful in such a context, schools must be providers of an innovative curriculum which is highly adaptable to changing needs, and, therefore, leaders must take up the challenge of developing a school climate which is conducive to learning, focuses on improvement rather than maintenance, encourages experimentation and innovation, and facilitates continuous teacher learning. This means that leaders in schools in the 1990s must embrace new ways of thinking and working based around collaborative patterns of personal leadership which will reculture their school into one of success.

In April 1992, at the time this research was completed, the Victorian government school system had been undergoing evolutionary change in devolution of authority from the centralized bureaucracy to the school level. School councils were engaging in participative, collaborative decision-making processes involving the whole school community, namely, teachers, parents and students (at secondary level) and sharing responsibility for determining their own curricula within the principles and framework of government policy. Regional boards of education had been established as a mechanism for collective decision-making between the school, the region and the central Ministry of Education. Education regions were viewed as collections of schools and schooling services in specific geographical areas. The schools in this study were located in one such region of the Victoria's Ministry of Education, each functioning through its own school council. It is important to note that since that time massive school reform has taken place in terms of the devolution of authority to Victorian government schools, now known as Schools of the Future, however these reforms are not the subject of this book.

To fully understand the context in which these school leaders were operating, a little background is necessary. The school communities where the research was undertaken were located in Melbourne which is the capital city of the state of Victoria, situated on the south-eastern coast of the continent. It is a large cosmopolitan city with a population of over three million people of diverse ethnic mix, backgrounds ranging from Asian, Middle-Eastern to European, as well as Australian. Inner Melbourne suburbs are traditional stopping off points for new arrivals to the city. They are densely populated, and provide a mix of residential, commercial, entertainment and industrial districts. Melbourne celebrates its multicultural character with festivals and entertainment, markets, restaurants and foods of every nationality. The inner areas of Melbourne are colourful places to live, and being in close proximity to the central business district, also attract numbers of students, professionals and academics as residents. The schools in inner city Melbourne reflect this population in its schools and it is from this context that the research for this book is taken.

School Success

A dizzying array of interpretations of 'success' has been put forward in educational circles, peppered with terms such as 'efficiency', 'effectiveness', 'excellence', 'quality', 'standards', 'performance' and so on. Success has most often been equated with academic test scores, especially those of the 'basic' skills of numeracy and literacy. Some will see success measured by the numbers of students who compete successfully in the workplace. Others will perceive it as a measure of the happiness and well-being of the person as a whole. Those in schools know that there is much in education that cannot be measured. Some of the most admirable learning is intangible and unquantifiable. However, whatever the definition one applies to success, it must include a set goal or objective, with the measure of success being gauged against its achievement.

In the context of this book, success is associated with effective school improvement. Wideen, in Fullan and Hargreaves (1992:123), indicates that understandings of what constitutes school success in school improvement are still in their infancy. Generally, however, success in school improvement is related to the organizational good health of a school with indicators of success conceived of as performance indicators. These are linked to school outcomes, and 'may be utilized in making judgments about aspects of a program, a program as a whole or the school as a whole, including the extent to which matters of fundamental importance in the school charter have been addressed, policies have been implemented or the development plan has progressed' (Caldwell and Spinks, 1992:148). For the purposes of this book, the following indicators of success in schools were employed:

- outstanding improvements in outcomes in recent years, in the program of the school as a whole or in one or more aspects of the program;
- success in the introduction of new approaches to learning and teaching, or the organization and support of learning and teaching;
- success in addressing a particular problem or set of problems;
- sustained achievement over many years.

How was it then that these five schools set about achieving success? What was it that they actually did in their schools to make it happen? What *sort* of leadership enabled success to be achieved despite the odds? In order to gain insight to such questions, a pressing need emerged to learn about *leadership* itself – what was *really* meant by that much-used term?

Two sources gave insights. The prime source was understandings gained from a comprehensive review of the current related theory and research. The second source was an exploratory study undertaken in two inner city Melbourne schools. The latter affirmed the need for the ensuing research and gave impetus to further investigation. A detailed account of the related theory and research will be presented in the next chapter. What follows is a brief overview of the exploratory study and its implications for this investigation.

The Exploratory Investigation

An exploratory study of two urban schools was undertaken prior to this study. Valuable information about the nature of leadership in urban schools was acquired and the findings indicated that a more comprehensive inquiry was well justified.

Findings at the two schools in the exploratory investigation indicated strong connections between collaborative cultures and success. The Waratah Primary School exhibited achievement in the areas of outstanding outcomes in recent years in the program of the school as a whole and success in the introduction of new approaches to teaching and learning. A significant and major achievement at Wattle Secondary College was success in addressing a particular problem, namely, 'racist behaviour, which continually plagued the efficient operation of the school community' (Debney Park High School, 1986:7) and centred around the development of a Human Rights Policy. As a result school programs were able to operate successfully.

The culture of each school was characterized by several central elements. At Waratah Primary School these were commitment (a people focus), vision, celebration, optimism, excellence, energy, networks, empowerment, flexibility and social justice values. At Wattle Secondary College collaboration, caring and concern, consultation, clear communication and guidelines, networking, listening, support, showing respect for all and valuing people, initiative and taking responsibility, a pragmatic realism, and flexibility and adaptability formed the essential characteristics. It would seem that, whilst there are underpinning similarities in the cultures of each of these schools, there are differences associated with the context in which the schools were operating at the particular time. For instance, Waratah Primary School was dealing with issues dominated by a transient, low socio-economic, non-English speaking background student population. The fundamental concerns at Wattle Secondary College related to the management of racial tensions between ethnic groups, and the recognition that these were impeding the processes of learning.

The elements of school culture derived from the findings of the exploratory study were depicted in hypothesized causal maps and are represented in Figures 1 and 2.

Of specific interest to this book are the areas of:

– consultation
– a people focus
– empowerment
– collaboration

The depth and breadth of successful achievement at the Waratah Primary School and Wattle Secondary College are reflected in the outstanding outcomes in the programs of the schools as a whole. There has been success in the introduction of new approaches to learning and teaching; success in the organization and support of the technical culture; and success in dealing constructively with the particular challenges facing urban schools. The nature of these findings had a critical influence in stimulating the thinking behind this book.

Figure 1: Hypothesized causal map of leadership and school outcomes at the Waratah Primary School

Figure 2: Causal network for development of the human rights policy for Wattle Secondary College

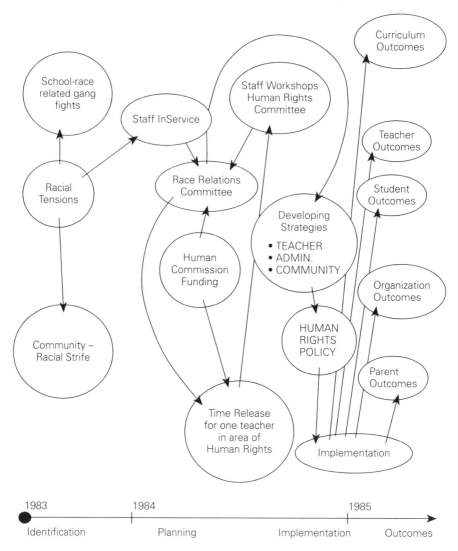

The next chapter is devoted entirely to the related theory and research which surrounds the concept of *leadership*. Particular attention is given to leadership theory as it relates to schools in the 1990s and to the ideas of Bolman and Deal (1991) proffered in their publication *Reframing Organisations: Artistry, Choice and Leadership* who propose the notion of viewing leadership through four frames – structural, human resource, political and symbolic.

Chapter 1

Leadership: Related Theory and Research

Leadership Theory

Leadership is defined in many ways. Stogdill (1974:259) wrote that 'there are almost as many definitions as there are persons who have attempted to define the concept.' Bennis and Nanus (1985) reported finding over 350 definitions in the literature and since then many more have been added. Burns (1978:18) tells us that 'leadership over human beings is exercised when persons with certain purposes mobilize, in competition or conflict with others, institutional, political, psychological and other resources so as to arouse, engage and satisfy the motives of the followers.' Sergiovanni (1987:2) believes that 'leadership is the process of persuasion by which a leader or leadership group (such as the state) induces followers to act in a manner that enhances the leader's purposes or shared purposes.' Greenfield (1986:142) describes leadership as 'a wilful act where one person attempts to construct the social world for others.' Beare, Caldwell and Millikan (1989:123) point out that 'leadership is concerned with gaining commitment to a set of values, statements of "what ought to be", which then become the heart of the culture of the school.' So before proceeding it is necessary to clarify exactly what is meant by the term *leadership* in the context of this book.

Since time began humans have sought out individuals whom it was felt would provide a superior wisdom which might bring sense and direction to their imperfect world. It was believed, or hoped, that some kind of ascending insight or intelligence could capture the elusive truth about the nature of humankind. These individuals, possessing, it was thought, exclusive character traits, would guide us to realms of understanding not known before. Such individuals were known as leaders and they were endowed with innate character traits which especially fitted them for their leadership roles, such as intelligence, initiative, self-assurance, enthusiasm, sociability, integrity and courage (Handy, 1985:94ff). Early research produced no conclusive evidence that these personal characteristics correlated with effective leadership, namely, leadership which generated desired outcomes. However, Stogdill (1974) has indicated that more recent studies have yielded such testimony: traits like energy, persistence, capacity to handle stress, sense of responsibility, risk-taking, and concern for task completion are seen to be attributes which characterize successful leaders. But trait theories 'rest on the assumption that the individual is more important than the situation' (Handy, 1985:93) in determining successful leadership, denying the complexities of the leadership milieu and not really getting to the bottom of what makes the difference between effective and ineffective leadership in a variety of situations.

Over the past half century a body of knowledge about leadership in education has developed. It began with Taylor's (1911) classical view that saw leadership predominantly as a matter of hierarchical power over subordin- ates and a primary concern with the task at hand (Mintzberg, 1973). Human relations proponents (Follett, 1941; McGregor, 1960) focused on people in organizations seeing leadership as interaction between leaders and others in the group. Behaviourists (Barnard, 1938) advocated leadership as both people- and task-oriented. Contingency views of leadership (Fiedler, 1967; Hersey and Blanchard, 1982) proposed that no one leadership approach could be claimed as *the* most effective; successful leadership was contextual. Political dimensions of power, conflict and morality have been addressed (Ball, 1987; Hoyle, 1986). Perspectives of gender and change theory also make their contribution. Each has been a response to the shortfalls of its predecessor in an attempt to dis- cover the full actuality encompassed by that elusive concept *leadership.*

In 1978 James McGregor Burns made an enlightening distinction between *transactional* and *transforming* leadership, providing a major shift in the think- ing behind leadership theory, particularly with regard to leadership and its connection with moral dimensions. Burns identifies two ways in which leader- ship is commonly exercised. Transactional leadership is primarily concerned with individuals within an organization negotiating their individual, as opposed to group, interests with the leader where both leader and staff are mutually satisfied with the arrangement. Transforming leadership, on the other hand, 'involves an exchange among people seeking common aims, uniting them to go beyond their separate interests in the pursuit of higher goals' (Sergiovanni and Starratt, 1988:198) in the way that Mahatma Ghandi, Martin Luther King and Jesus Christ inspired others to a shared commitment of their vision (Burns, 1978). Sergiovanni (1987:6) contends that :

> In transformational leadership, by contrast [to transactional leader- ship], regardless of special interest and goals, administrators and teachers are united in pursuit of higher level goals that are common to both. Both, for example, want to become the best. Both want to shape the school in a new direction.

Unlike early notions of individual leadership, transforming leadership (re- ferred to as the more widespread concept of transformational leadership) acknowledges that in today's challenging and demanding educational climate of constant and turbulent change, no single person alone is likely to have the combined capacities necessary to engage in effective leadership. And it can be legitimately argued, that in empowering a range of people within the school community – teachers, students, parents and others as appropriate – a combined richness of educational thought and activity, superior to that of any single leader, can be achieved. That is, leadership at its best is a shared venture engaged in by many. Further, as Louis and Miles (1991) point out, if implementation of vision is to be effective, then power sharing is critical. Louis and Miles' (1991) research indicates that leaders in successful schools are able to support the initiative-taking of others, be it teachers, parents or students, without fear of losing control; facilitate the formation of teams and working parties; resource these initiatives; at the same time keeping in close touch with the groups and monitoring their progress. Sergiovanni (1987:122) refers to 'the extent to which leadership roles are shared and the extent to which leadership is broadly exercised' as 'leadership density'. With a spread of leadership in the school, the principal is freed to take a more constructive role, as Fullan and Hargreaves (1991b:15) note, 'from that of a meeting-bound bureaucrat, to an instructional leader who can work closely with his or her staff in developing and implementing common educational goals.'

Sergiovanni (1984:6) advanced insight into the leadership theory debate when he classified leadership perspectives into five 'leadership forces', incorporating the two-dimensional task and relationship perspectives which had dominated the previous decades of research, renaming them *technical* and *human* forces, and adding three further dimensions – *educational, symbolic* and *cultural*. The technical, human and educational leadership forces combine to accomplish effectiveness in schools, but if excellence is to be achieved then, Sergiovanni argues, it is necessary to focus on symbolic and cultural forces. Technical and human elements address the management competencies of the organization; the educational dimension serves to ensure the effectiveness of the teaching and learning in the school; and symbolic and cultural perspectives take account of the need to go beyond competent management to higher values – purposes which bring about a desired better state of affairs through vision and the building of a strong school culture. Sergiovanni's five forces of leadership are as follows:

- *technical* – accomplishing the tasks of the organization [planning, organizing, coordinating, commanding and controlling];
- *human* – attending to human factors [consideration of relationships among people in the organization, morale, empowerment];
- *educational* – instructional leadership [addressing educational problems, developing and evaluating curriculum, professional development];
- *symbolic* – capacity of leaders to create, communicate and gain commitment to a vision [to impart purpose, values and significance, utilize symbols]; and
- *cultural* – capacity to build a strong school culture [to generate shared values and beliefs and a strong commitment to the organization].

Bennis and Nanus (1985) explored the notion of 'vision' and applied it to the leadership discussion. Their book identified ninety exceptional leaders and showed that successful leaders are able to focus attention on vision, communicate the vision through symbols and rhetoric, and due to their strength of personal commitment, see the vision through into practice. This has direct relevance to Sergiovanni's *symbolic* force of leadership.

The development of the concepts of transformational leadership, the five forces of leadership, vision, and empowerment, have all been influential in the work of current leadership theorists. Drawing on all these perspectives, Starratt (1988:213) has developed an insightful model of leadership known as the 'communal institutionalizing of vision', where, Starratt contends, if schools are to be successful, leadership must be transforming, translating vision into the daily operation of educational activities through shared processes.

School Leadership in the 1990s

Leadership – A Definition

Yukl (1989:252) proposes a definition of leadership which attempts to capture the elusive qualities of the concept: 'Leadership is defined broadly [as] influencing task objectives and strategies, influencing commitment and compliance in task behaviour to achieve these objectives, influencing group maintenance and identification, and influencing the culture of an organization.' Yukl's definition is one which embraces a composite of the notions of leadership density, multi-dimensional leadership forces, the institutionalization of vision; and one which favours transformational rather than transactional leadership. Embracing the notion of leadership density has significant implications for the definition of a 'leader'. It signals the extent to which leadership can pervade an organization. It takes account of both formal and informal leadership influences, and it allows for a rich network of influences to be sanctioned in addition to the formal hierarchical ones. Given this, who then *are* the leaders in a school? Who holds the influence and authority on behalf of the school community? The answer lies in the individual people in the school itself and their potential for participating in constructive leadership activity. In other words there is no limit to who can be a leader; the only limitation is the limitations of the people themselves. I would like to propose as broad a base as possible for leadership in the school, and so for the purposes of this investigation a leader can be a principal, a teacher, a parent, a student, a supporting staff member, such as a multicultural aide, *as long as* they have the capacity, referred to by Yukl, to 'influenc[e] task objectives and strategies, influenc[e] commitment and compliance in task behaviour to achieve these objectives, influenc[e] group maintenance and identification, and influenc[e] the culture of an organization.' Any member of the school community who demonstrates such capabilities is defined in this book as a *leader*. To this extent, leadership is not necessarily hierarchical, but inclusive of all those who comply with Yukl's criteria and who wish to contribute.

Closely linked to the notion of leadership density is the concept of transformational leadership. Transformational leadership initiates a transformation in the school and has particular connotations for school improvement and success. A feature of this transformation is that it is accomplished by a density of leadership across the school, through empowered leaders of the school community. Critical to achieving success is the fact that the vision of the school is *shared* by all the leaders so that its implementation ranges across a wide scope of influence. When the vision becomes widely grounded in the routine activities of the school, it is known as *institutionalization of vision.*

The concept of leadership developed in the conceptual framework of this book is one which takes account of a multi-dimensional view of leadership. It encompasses Sergiovanni's (1984) five forces of leadership (technical, human, educational, symbolic, cultural), Sergiovanni and Starratt's (1988) notion of institutionalizing vision, and includes Bolman and Deal's (1991) reorganization of the key concepts embodied in the accumulated leadership theory into the categories of structural, human resource, political and symbolic dimensions.

Leadership, then, is seen here as drawing upon Yukl's definition outlined above, and as *transformational*, embracing a composite of the notions of leadership density, multi-dimensional leadership forces, and the institutionalization of vision.

Transformational as Opposed to Transactional Leadership

This book sets out to untangle and clarify our conception of leadership, or at least what our own perception of leadership might be. To me this perception is of fundamental significance, guiding the way leaders operate in their schools. Whilst most of the current literature espouses *transformational* leadership as the enlightened way to achieve school success in practice as in theory, there is often a lack of commitment to the key features which are integral to its materialization. At the theoretical level, conceptual differences of belief as to what transformational leadership *is*, present a serious quandary. For, example, Leithwood's paper presented at the Seventh International Congress for School Effectiveness and Improvement in 1994 describes a form of two-factor transformational leadership as a composite of transactional and transformational elements, including the transactional notion of 'contingent reward' where 'the leader tells staff what to do in order to be rewarded for their efforts' (Leithwood, 1994:9). Gronn's (1995:14) rendition of the model of the transformational leader 'as a resurrected version and virtually defunct leader type . . . the hero or great leader' conveys another conceptual interpretation. Gronn (1995:25) equates Bass's conception of transformational leadership with a rugged type of individualism and suggests that it 'carries with it all the hallmarks of a religious crusade and being born again'. Leithwood and Gronn appear to attach meanings of *individual leadership* to the notion of transformational leadership and futher imply a subordinate relationship between leader and staff. It would seem a serious conceptual shift from Burns' definition of transformational leadership has been made by both Leithwood and Gronn, moving away from the notion of *group* exchange to *individual* exchange. In Burns' meaning, the position posed by Leithwood in his 1994 paper, and Gronn in his 1995 article, is that of *transactional*, not transformational, leadership. Burns' (1978) central proposition on transformational leadership involves members of an organization pursuing *shared* beliefs, *through combined efforts*, overriding their individual interests in the quest for the common good (see p.11). This aligns with the position presented in this book where critical significance is given to *collaboration of the whole school community*, or its nominated representatives, as the underpinning constituent leading to school success. The notion of leadership density, where teachers (and others) become empowered to take on the role of leaders, and *jointly* undertake the institutionalization of the school's vision, is fundamental to the notion of collaboration. The focus of this book strenuously proposes that Burns' distinction between transactional and transformational leadership be adopted, for if leadership is to be truly collaborative, group purposes are fundamental to its success, rather than transactional exchange between leader and the led.

Further, Gronn's likening of transformational leadership to a religious crusade overstates and glamorizes the reality of work in schools, and, I daresay, organizations in general. Being a leader in a school in the 1990s is no picnic. There are no loaves and fishes here. Just plain hard work, dedication and a firm desire to do the right thing for the young people and families in our collective care. This is done by putting our heads together and discussing, challenging, brainstorming, arguing and problem-solving our way through the issues, steadfastly and resolutely. The reality of what is happening in schools is this – *we do not have the answer about how to proceed. We do not know, nor does anyone else.* However, we do know that what is needed is improvement, not maintenance. What then do we do? Do we wait for a prophet, religious or charismatic, to appear from on high? The related theory and research of the past fifty years, and best practice of the 1990s, indicates otherwise, for it plainly tells us that *no single person alone has the combined capacity to do the job.*

At the practical level, where *individual* transactions (as Leithwood seems to be suggesting), albeit judicious or innovative ones between the principal or senior staff are the norm, can bring disastrous results. I speak in such strong terms as my own experience has brought some salutary lessons to bear on this front. I have witnessed transactional leadership causing the undoing of many leaders and the downfall of several good schools, as it unwittingly brings about a negative school culture where confusion, distrust, lack of cooperation and even dissent prevail. Such a culture is not conducive to a successful teaching and learning environment, nor to the educational well-being of students. Positive school cultures are hard won, but they are darned easy to lose. There is a surprising fragility in an organization's state of good health and its condition can deteriorate swiftly if the *modus operandi* is one which relies on individual, rather than collective, negotiation and decision-making. If we want to improve our organizations we must work together in a focused way, as parts of a single entity, to identify and achieve the purposes critical to making classrooms real places of learning for our students. The prophet has already arrived and is amongst us, but not in the shape of the singular form – *in the plural*. This is the essence of transformative leadership. It centres around workgroups of committed professionals who, with shared and directed purpose, have the capacity to work together in a problem-solving way to determine tentative answers to the unknown, to take action on the basis of what they have discovered, and move on. In doing so they make schools better places to be; places of continuing learning for both themselves and their students.

As far as *ideal* leadership *per se* goes, it is stressed that we have not arrived at *the* answer, and the struggle to come closer to it proceeds forward as it has in the past, and will continue to do in the future. However, there are few amongst us, I would venture to say, who are not striving for an understanding of doing a better job as a leader in their school, and few who do not aspire to making a constructive difference in the educational setting in which they work. Crusaders will not make a difference, collaborators will. Transformational, not transactional, leadership is required if schools are to become the places we want them to be, and if we are to lead them successfully into the unchartered waters ahead. The following chapters present one version of how this might be done and seek to advance our understanding of what can be done.

The Bolman and Deal Framework

Clearly an explicit and precise conception of *what transformational leadership is* needs to be delineated. The latter part of this chapter details Bolman and Deal's (1991) approach, for it is that approach which has been adopted to form the structural, human resource, political and symbolic framework around which leadership in the participating schools has been investigated. Using this analytical tool, and drawing heavily on the related leadership literature summarized previously, the concept of transformational leadership is explored in its collaborative mode, and elements of collaboration across the four frames are extracted to formulate an operational definition of *collaborative leadership*. The following section of this chapter provides a means by which a clear and succinct clarification of transformational leadership can be advanced; one which has the potential to avoid inherent confusion and misinterpretation.

The previous section of this chapter sets out in some detail the definitions and distinctions surrounding the notion of leadership in the context of schools in the 1990s. Implicit in these definitions and distinctions is the understanding that leadership has many dimensions. Bolman and Deal in their 1991 publication, *Reframing Organisations: Artistry, Choice and Leadership*, suggest a reorganization of the key concepts embodied in the accumulated body of leadership theory into what they call four *frames*. These four frames classify what is currently known about leadership into four categories – structural, human resource, political and symbolic – providing a framework for understanding and decoding the leadership milieu of a school or organization. The structural frame emphasizes the importance of formal roles and relationships where the focus is on organizational direction and goals, roles, policies, procedures, coordination and planning. The human resource frame acknowledges that organizations are inhabited by individuals whose talents, skills and energy are the organization's most valuable resource. Effective leadership takes account of this, arranging structures and conditions to meet professional and personal needs of staff. The political frame addresses the political realities of an organization. Used wisely, political power is seen as a constructive and necessary part of the leadership function. The symbolic frame tunes into the non-rational aspect of organizational activity decoding embedded beliefs, values, attitudes and norms of behaviour of the organizational culture. Bolman and Deal (1991) advocate a strategy called 'framing' which ensures that any analysis of leadership is one which incorporates all contingencies and complexities across the four frames, thereby taking account of the composite of leadership understandings.

Framing

Bolman and Deal describe their concept of *framing*:

> The perspectives, or frames . . . are based on four major schools of organizational theory and research and we have outlined the central assumptions and propositions of each of them . . . Our goal is useable knowledge . . . Each of these frames has its own vision or image of reality. Only when managers, consultants, and policy-makers can look through all four are they likely to appreciate the depth and complexity of organizational life (Bolman and Deal, 1991:14–16).

Drawing on Erving Goffman's (1974) seminal work on frame theory, Bolman and Deal (1991) explain how four frames of leadership enlarge the focus of leaders' thinking to bring a more versatile and artistic dimension to organizational practice. Key concepts drawn from existing organizational theory – cultural, symbolic, educational, human and technical – have been consolidated and reorganized into the structural, human resource, political and symbolic frames, providing a framework on which to interpret, analyse and understand what is happening in an organization. Bolman and Deal's notion of framing relates to all organizations, drawing on examples from the business and the public sector, as well as from education. The full picture of organizational complexity, Bolman and Deal suggest (1991:xv), will remain elusive unless all angles are taken into consideration. Use of the four frames enable 'managerial freedom and leadership effectiveness' by looking at the same situation in an organization in four different ways – structural, human resource, political and symbolic. A narrow, simplistic view is thus avoided and, instead, some real sense of the organizational milieu is realized and can be acted upon. Bolman and Deal caution leaders to be aware of their preferred perspectives (frames) and its overuse to the detriment of alternative ones. 'People who understand their own frame – and who have learnt to rely on more than one perspective – are better equipped to understand and manage the complex everyday world of organizations' (Bolman and Deal, 1991:14). Ability to move in and out of the four frames brings deeper insights and a broadening of horizons, allowing eclectic use of the current, composite body of theoretical knowledge. Reframing, then, is a process of thorough, active, practical analysis and implementation of leadership theory.

Each frame is based on a body of knowledge drawn from contributing disciplines. The structural frame, rooted in sociology, focuses on the formal structure and operations of the school; the human resource frame draws on organizational social psychology, addressing the skills and needs of educators; the political frame, has its origin in political science, centering on the political relations of power in the school community; and the symbolic frame is founded in social and cultural anthropology, focusing on values and beliefs of the people in an organization and the culture in which they reside. Bolman and Deal maintain that, whilst all these bodies of knowledge have a legitimate contribution to make, each has its own assumptions about how schools and people work together. 'Each body of theory purports to rest on a scientific foundation. But theories are often theologies that preach only one version of the scripture' (Bolman and Deal, 1991:10). The combined use, therefore, of all 'theologies' through the use of the four frames brings a complete picture which otherwise may remain wanting.

The Structural Frame

The structural frame emphasizes the importance of formal roles and rela- tionships. 'Structures – commonly depicted by means of organizational charts – are created to fit an organisation's environment and technology' (Bolman and Deal, 1991:15). The focus is on organizational direction and goals, roles, policies, procedures and co-ordination and planning. The structural processes in the school provide the vehicle by which clarification of direction, roles and documentation of policies and procedures can be communicated and under- taken and, therefore, is a means by which the vision of the school is put into practice.

Caldwell and Spinks' (1988) model offers an example of a structural frame- work for whole school planning where organizational direction, roles, policies and procedures are coordinated and systematically managed, through a pro- cess of collaboration which:

- integrates goal-setting, policy-making, planning, budgeting, imple- menting and evaluating in a manner which contrasts with the often unsystematic, fragmented processes which have caused so much frustration and ineffectiveness in the past;

- secures appropriate involvement of staff, students and the community, with clearly defined roles for governing bodies where such groups exist and have responsibility for policy-making;
- focuses on the central functions of schools – learning and teaching – and, accordingly, organizes the management of the school around 'programmes' which correspond to the preferred patterns of work in the school (Caldwell and Spinks, 1988:3).

The model contains the six phases of goal-setting and need identification, policy-making, planning and programs, preparation and approval of program budgets, and implementing and evaluating. Here it is advocated that the goals and needs of the school are kept to the fore when policy-making and planning take place. An updated version (Caldwell and Spinks, 1992:33) adds the element of culture into the model, and provides guidelines for leaders for shaping a strong culture in their schools. Such structural arrangements are integral to leadership in schools, and take into account Sergiovanni's (1984) technical force of leadership.

The Human Resource Frame

The human resource frame is underpinned by the premise that schools are social organizations steeped in human needs, wants and claims (Argyris, 1984; Owens, 1991). There is constant interplay between the individual and the organization to ensure a fit between administrative goals and individual members. If organizations are alienating in their operation, valuable human talents are lost and human lives become unfulfilled (Deal, 1990). Effective leadership takes account of the fact that people and organizations need each other. Organizations need professional experience and expertise, ideas and commitment; people need satisfying work, an income and social and personal expression. Good leadership is sensitive to this interdependence, arranging structures and conditions to meet the professional and personal needs of staff.

The quality of the decisions which are made, and the improved outcomes for students that result from them, will depend on the extent to which leaders operate over the broad base of all those who are directly responsible for the education of the students in the school, including teachers, students, parents and other members of the school community. Genuine involvement in school decision-making acknowledges and values the collective skills and expertise of all within the organization, believing each can contribute meaningfully in their own way. Participatory decision-making ensures that those responsible for implementing decisions or policies are actively engaged in the decision-making process itself; not in a one-off or occasional capacity but as a continuous, on-going and integral part of daily school operations. As well, teachers need to have the opportunity for professional learning and development in a context that is at once supportive and challenging. Drawing on such human resources strengthens the educational environment for our children. Leithwood (1992:96) explains, 'principals look below the surface features of their schools – at how teachers are treated and what beliefs, norms and values they share – and redesign their schools as learning environments for teachers as well as for students.'

The Political Frame

According to Bolman and Deal (1991:187), 'the political frame asserts that in the face of enduring differences and scarce resources, conflict among members of a coalition is inevitable and power incidentally becomes a resource.' Political behaviour is an inevitable consequence of a social organization and includes, as Robbins (1989:353) states, 'those activities that are not required as part of one's formal role in the organisation but that influence, or attempt to influence, the distribution of advantages and disadvantages within the organisation.'

Political tactics need not bear negative connotations. Used wisely political power is a constructive and necessary part of the leadership function. Leaders use power as a means of attaining group goals and facilitating achievements. Solutions to problems can be developed through political skill and acumen. Negotiation and bargaining are all part of everyday organizational life. If, as Bolman and Deal (1991) suggest, the goals, structure and policies of a school emerge from an ongoing process of bargaining and negotiating among staff, then there is a pressing need for leaders to be active in the political process.

Given the social nature of schools and the fact that the entire educational enterprise revolves around people, political behaviour is inescapable. As Robbins (1989:339) states 'the acquisition and distribution of power is a natural process in any group or organisation.' Here political realities are recognized and 'human beings live out their daily lives and socially construct their reality through the negotiations, contractions and resistances of the rules and resources within which their lives are entwined' (Watkins, 1989:23).

The Symbolic Frame

The concept of culture has had a central role in the leadership debate. Leaders in schools know they must work simultaneously on staff needs and skills, on goals and roles and the dynamics of political power and conflict. But there is something that operates beyond all these, an intangible manifestation that reflects the ethos or climate of a school. This tapestry that is woven into the fabric of the organization is known as its culture. Sergiovanni (1984) delineates a cultural leadership force as developing shared values and purposes. Deal and Peterson (1990:7) describe school culture:

This invisible, taken-for-granted flow of beliefs and assumptions gives meaning to what people say and do. It shapes how they interpret hundreds of daily transactions. This deeper structure of life in organizations is reflected and transmitted through symbolic language and expressive action. Culture consists of the stable, underlying social meanings that shape belief and behaviour over time.

This conglomerate of beliefs, values, attitudes and norms of behaviour are embedded in the activities of school life and are represented in the symbols, rituals and ceremonies of the school. Deal and Kennedy (1982) advanced the thinking on school culture, writing of heroes and myths, demons, rituals and ceremonies which wield a powerful influence behind the rationality of organizational management. As Starratt (1993:5) states:

Leadership in the cultural perspective is exercized not so much by scientific management as by guarding essential values of the culture, by reminding people in the organization of the essential meanings of the culture, by promoting rituals and celebrations which sustain those essential meanings and values.

The symbolic frame is a means of *decoding* the culture. It tunes into the non-rational aspect of organizational activity. However, in terms of conceptualizing the symbolic perspective, it is important to distinguish it from the notion of culture. In many writings associated with leadership theory, culture is seen as synonymous with values, beliefs, shared meanings, symbols, rituals and ceremonies. Whilst acknowledging that the two are closely aligned, the position taken here is that symbolic aspects do not *equal* culture. In this book, collaborative culture is interpreted in a broader context which importantly *includes* the symbolic frame, but also embraces structural, human resource and political perspectives. This distinction is a critical one, for it lies at the heart of a broader conceptualization of the notion of collaboration, and, indeed, culture. Exactly what is meant by this will be the subject of the following chapter. Initially discussion will be given to the culture of a school; more specifically emphasis will focus on a collaborative culture. From this theoretical background, elements of collaborative leadership will be identified and an operational definition developed.

Chapter 2

Collaborative Leadership

This chapter sets out to make some meaning of what collaborative leadership is *in practice*, namely, what collaborative leaders *do* in their schools to achieve success for students, teachers and the organization itself. In this book, the notion of collaborative leadership is extended into structural, human resource and political domains, *in addition to* symbolic perspectives, providing a fuller picture and a more comprehensive base for interpretation of the leadership milieu. As with collaborative leadership, this extended view has direct implications for the notion of a collaborative *culture* of a school, for instead of viewing culture as purely symbolic in its roots, it can be seen as inclusive of structural, human resource and political dimensions. This broader conceptual framework has been developed to act as a guide for leaders in their daily practice. However, before discussing it further, a brief account follows of the related research undertaken so far in the field of collaboration. Authors have given much attention to describing collaborative cultures in schools and this brings significant and pertinent findings and offer insights of value in this study.

Setting the Background of Collaboration in Schools

Traditional school cultures were based on norms of professional isolation and autonomy (Goodlad, 1984; Johnson, 1990; Lortie, 1975). These cultures had their place in schools where narrow academic expectations prevailed, parents made a significant contribution to the education of students, school leaders were not required to act as instructional leaders, accountability was unimportant, community relationships were weak and there were few external pressures for change; teaching was seen as a craft with limited need for technical knowledge. As these circumstances no longer exist in the majority of schools, and are especially alien to urban schools, it is not surprising that a different culture in schools is emerging, broadly termed a collaborative culture.

Early studies of collaboration at the school level were generated by the pioneering work of Dan Lortie (1975) whose research centred on teachers – what they valued and how their workplace functioned. Lortie's work, *School Teacher: A Sociological Book*, revealed that the cellular organization of schools separates teachers from their colleagues, resulting in professional isolation. As a result, norms of not sharing their professional work develop, and a common culture is inhibited. Teachers are student-centred and their primary interest lies in the classroom, with the needs of children and how best to address them. However, uncertainty characterizes the mood of teachers, who are not sure whether or not they have had an influence on their students, or, indeed, whether they live up to the expectations of a 'good' teacher. Lortie's studies have been confirmed in numerous other inquiries (Clark and Yinger, 1977; House and Lapan, 1978; Huberman, 1983). Further research followed. Little (1982a) investigated why it was that schools where collegial exchange took place were such a rarity. Goodlad's (1984) analysis of the context in which teacher work substantiated the theme of autonomous isolation. What is of concern here is the quality of what was being taught, and the way in which it was being delivered to students, if left solely to individual teachers who have little or no professional contact in their schools.

More recent studies have investigated the phenomenon of collaboration as opposed to isolation. Two of particular note were completed and published in 1989, one by Susan Rosenholtz in the United States, the other by Jennifer Nias, Geoff Southworth and Robin Yeomans in the United Kingdom. Rosenholtz's *Teachers' Workplace: The Social Organization Of Schools* gives an enlightening account of the collaborative work environments of thirteen 'moving' or 'learning-enriched' primary schools in Tennessee. Her main book contends that learning-enriched schools, in contrast to learning-impoverished schools, are characterized by a collaborative culture which engenders shared goals, staff norms of continuous learning and mutual support and technical confidence of teachers, directly resulting in high teacher commitment and improved student learning. Rosenholtz labels schools with strong levels of collaboration, in which teachers have a common purpose and work openly and cooperatively, as 'high-consensus' schools and tells us they are distinguished by a sense of cohesion and community. As well, 'high consensus and forward-moving schools were marked by a spirit of continuous improvement in which no teacher ever stopped learning how to teach' (Rosenholtz, 1989:xi). What this means in practice is that a collaborative environment makes it possible for *all* staff to work unselfconsciously together as a team, despite all their differences, sharing a common goal, to be collectively responsible for its attainment and to help each other towards it.

Nias and her colleagues in their book, *Staff Relationships in the Primary School*, give a thorough account of the collaborative cultures of five English primary schools, already noted for their positive staff relationships. The authors taught and worked in the schools for a year and produced findings which showed that collaboration is immersed in the very culture of a school. They proposed that what characterized the collaborative workplace in the schools in their project was a dominant culture of shared values, beliefs and understandings which were arrived at through informal personal interactions. Nias, *et al.*, (1989:208) describe collaboration in schools:

. . . in the choreography of collaborative schools, norms of self-reliance appeared to be selfish infractions against school community. With teaching defined as inherently difficult, many minds tended to work better together than the few. Here requests for and offers of advice and assistance seemed more like moral imperatives, and colleagues seldom acted without foresight and deliberate calculation. Teacher leaders were identified as those who reached out to each other with encouragement, technical knowledge to solve classroom problems, and enthusiasm for learning new things.

This collaborative work culture acknowledges and values the interdependence of the individual and the group in a school and effectively harnesses that balance of relationships so that, as Fullan and Hargreaves (1991:49) put it, 'the individual and the group are inherently and simultaneously valued.' As a consequence, teachers in this culture are empowered personally and collectively, acquiring a combined confidence which enables them to respond critically to the demands of the workplace.

In 1990, Susan Moore Johnson undertook her research in public and private schools of the eastern districts of Massachusetts in the United States. It was published in *Teachers Work: Achieving Success in Our Schools*. She interviewed over 100 highly respected teachers and discovered that good teachers were leaving the classroom because schools did not encourage an environment that stimulated good teaching. Her main contention was that good teaching requires a workplace which actively encourages collegiality and collaboration. She further maintains that schools, as they are presently organized, work against this and need to be restructured to allow for the kind of working environment which fosters cooperative teaching practice. These outcomes were confirmed by Yin Cheong Cheng (1993) in his paper on principal leadership in 190 primary schools in Hong Kong. Cheng reported that the principal's leadership is a critical factor for school performance at multi-levels. Cheng developed a 'measure of strong leadership' in which 'a principal can be supportive and foster participation for teachers, can develop clear goals and policies and hold people accountable for results, can be persuasive at building alliances and solving conflicts, can be inspirational and charismatic, and can encourage professional development and teaching improvement.' This 'strong' leadership is associated with high organizational effectiveness, strong organizational culture, positive principal–teacher relationships, more participation in decision-making, high teacher morale and professionalism, less teacher disengagement and hindrance, more teacher job satisfaction and commitment, and more positive student performance particularly on attitudes to their schools and learning (Cheng, 1993: abstract). Cheng's description of strong leadership provides a context for leadership which is relevant to this book, drawing as it does on structural, human, political, and symbolic dimensions advocated by Bolman and Deal (1991). The Australian Principals Associations Professional Development Council in their 1993 publication *Leaders and Their Learning: Professional*

Development Priorities for Principals (1993:37), noted a strong correlation between collaborative leadership and effective teacher development.

Studies of leadership in urban schools in the United States have been undertaken by Miles (1987), and in Canada by Fullan (1988) and Leithwood and Jantzi (1990). Miles' work was concerned with a broad focus on a number of factors associated with leadership and school improvement. Of particular interest to this book are the factors of empowerment and initiative-taking. Fullan's writings focus on school effectiveness, including studies of collegiality. Leithwood and Jantzi's (1990) research looks at transformational leadership in schools and the extent to which it develops collaborative cultures. Their inquiry strongly parallels the focus of this book. Leithwood and Jantzi systematically assessed the degree of collaboration in nine primary and three secondary urban schools noted for their significant improvement in Ontario, Canada, establishing connections between transformational leadership strategies and the development of collaborative cultures. Six broad strategies which were used by leaders to influence school cultures:

- strengthening the school's culture;
- use of a variety of bureaucratic mechanisms to stimulate and reinforce cultural change;
- fostering of staff development;
- engaging in direct and frequent communication about cultural norms, values and beliefs;
- shared power and responsibility with others; and
- use of symbols to express cultural values.

The foregoing research indicates that a culture of collegiality which simultaneously values, and caters to individual and group needs results in a collaborative workplace which will advance the teaching practice of a school, and, therefore, the enhancement of student learning. Fullan and Hargreaves (1991b:48) describe their interpretation of a fully functioning collaborative culture:

> What characterizes cultures of collaboration are not formal organization, meetings or bureaucratic procedures. Nor are cultures of collaboration mounted for specific projects and events. Rather, they consist of pervasive qualities, attitudes, and behaviours that run through staff relationships on a moment-by-moment, day-by-day basis. Help, support, trust and openness are at the heart of these relationships. Beneath that, there is a commitment to valuing people as individuals and valuing the groups to which people belong.

Fullan and Hargreaves' interpretation of a fully functioning collaborative culture falls short of the broader conceptualization presented in this book. It is an extremely apt description of the symbolic aspects of collaboration, but overlooks structural, human resource and political dimensions. Fullan and

Hargreaves' interpretation reflects mainstream thinking on the subject of collaboration. Therefore it is necessary to ask ourselves what collaboration is. In the absence of any formal definition in the preceding literature, an operational definition of collaboration must be developed in this chapter, based on findings from the related theory and research, and, importantly, centering around quite *specific and extensive collaborative elements* of leadership. These specific collaborative elements have been categorized into Bolman and Deal's four frames – structural, human resource, political and symbolic – in order to ensure the full range of potentialities and complexities of leadership have been embraced. This is a significant process as recent writings exploring the nature of collegiality have cautioned educators on its superficial or negative aspects (Fullan, 1993; Hargreaves and Dawe, 1990; Huberman, 1991; Little, 1990). The integration of the collaborative elements into the four frames forms a conceptual framework from which collaborative leadership behaviours can be viewed in an extended and comprehensive form, which is critical if a narrow focus is to be avoided.

At this point it is worth noting that collaboration is *one* aspect of transformational leadership. Chapter 1 documented the related literature surrounding the leadership discussion, and together with the findings of the Inner Melbourne Leadership Project's Exploratory investigation (Preface: IMLPE xi), many elements of leadership have been identified. However, this book has limited its focus to concepts specifically pertaining to elements of *collaborative* leadership, and has moved from transformational leadership in general, to collaborative leadership in particular.

Collaborative Leadership – A Conceptual Framework

The following elements emerge in a synthesis of findings in the review of related literature and the exploratory investigation, and are organized into the Bolman and Deal frames:

Elements of collaboration

structural frame
- democratic processes;
- leadership density;
- direction/vision;
- shared goals;
- shared responsibility;
- roles;
- policy processes;
- program procedures;

- coordination;
- planning;
- listening;
- frank, open and frequent communication.

human resource frame
- centrality of teaching and learning;
- strong sense of community;
- value and regard for professional development;
- teachers as curriculum leaders;
- parents as co-partners;
- teams;
- teachers teaching teachers;
- professional honesty;
- support, praise and trust;
- acceptance;
- sharing;
- continuous learning;
- continuous improvement;
- positive student/staff relations;
- staff cohesion.

political frame
- absence of hierarchy;
- power-sharing;
- open discussion;
- consensus;
- majority rule;
- shared responsibility;
- using authority;
- using influence;
- diffusing conflict;
- agreed-upon 'political' behaviour;
- participatory decision-making procedures;
- disagreements not seen as disruptive;
- absence of sub-groups;
- negotiation;
- coalitions;
- networks;
- frank, open and frequent communication.

symbolic frame
- beliefs;
- values;
- attitudes;
- norms of behaviour;

- shared meanings;
- symbols;
- rituals;
- ceremonies.

The categorization of these elements has been made in an attempt to rationalize what by very nature is an irrational context, namely the vigorously dynamic milieu of the day-to-day endeavours of a school. Each of the elements is inextricably linked and interrelated to each other. However, for the purposes of eliciting their cause and effect relationships, elements have been grouped and classified into the four frames. It is recognized that the elements may be categorized differently. Many combinations and permutations could legitimately be made. For example, *vision* has been included in the structural frame, where it denotes the clear direction which underlines and steers policy-making and implementation, planning, coordination and so on, all of which are critical to the inclusive nature of a structurally collaborative culture. On the other hand vision might be seen to naturally fall into the classification of the symbolic frame as it is so profoundly symbolic in character. For my purposes, however, the emphasis of the element of vision was to be one of overtly shared purposes which would translate the beliefs of the whole school community into the daily practice of the school. Conceptually, vision can be alternatively construed as personal in nature and somewhat covert in make-up. It is with the former characteristics that the notion of vision has been adopted for this book and has therefore been included in the structural frame.

Similarly, the element of listening could be interchangeably included in other frames depending on the emphasis required. Listening is an integral part of the participatory decision-making process (structural); listening brings about support or continuous improvement (human resource); listening is critical to open discussion or diffusing conflict (political); and, listening is implicit to a valuing of participation and an attitude of inclusiveness (symbolic). The interrelated nature of the elements in reality makes for a contrived and arbitrary separation. It is my view that any categorization is a necessary, but limiting, exercise to uncover the practical specifics of the causal connections of collaborative leadership. The critical factor is that within the composite of the interrelationships of elements, no matter where they are listed, each element is included and is a significant contributor to the whole. The cross connections and interchangeability of these elements are further evidence for the need of a definition which goes beyond the symbolic frame.

Collaborative Leadership – A Definition

An integration of the above collaborative elements into Bolman and Deal's four frames, have been combined to provide an operational definition of collaborative leadership. This definition is illustrated in Figure 3 below.

Figure 3: Elements of collaborative leadership

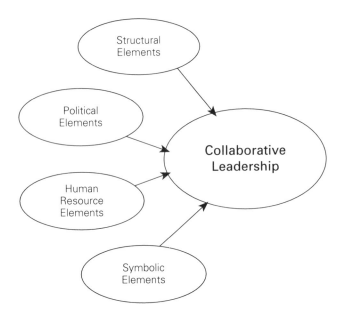

In Figure 3, the structural elements of leadership, which contribute to a collaborative leadership, refer to the way in which leaders structure decision-making processes to allow appropriate staff, student and parent participation such that a shared vision and agreed-upon ways of implementing the direction, policies and programs of the school can occur. In the exploratory investigation these were noted by a flat hierarchy, frank and open communication, listening, respecting and valuing people and empowerment.

Human resource elements refer to the professional development of staff through cooperative sharing of their collective experience. It assumes leaders foster an environment of mutual support, professional acceptance and continuous learning. It is characterized by a focus on the centrality of learning and teaching as the school's primary purpose and high levels of staff and student commitment.

Political elements of collaborative leader behaviour centre around reaching agreement through discussion, negotiation and compromise in a climate of openness. Disagreement and discord are expected in the social, value-laden context of the school. Rather than being seen as hindrances to successful practice, legitimate political processes are incorporated as part of everyday life, facilitating the attainment of shared goals and advancing the educational agenda.

Symbolic elements of a collaboration are characterized by deep-seated, often unspoken, shared beliefs, values and attitudes which bring about norms of interaction, friendly, informal staff relations and a pervasive camaraderie. Collaborative leaders value diversity, acceptance of differences, interpersonal openness and an atmosphere of genuine care, and concern for colleagues, personally and professionally is the norm. Rituals and ceremonies symbolize, and give visible presence to, symbolic perspectives. Structural, human resource, political and symbolic elements are all inextricably linked and interrelated. Their segregation into the four frames offers a focus for analysis and a means of making sense of what often seems to be an irrational and chaotic working world.

Summary

Fully functioning collaborative leadership ensures the vision of the school becomes, in Sergiovanni and Starratt's (1988:213) terms, 'institutionalized'. Collaborative leadership is transforming leadership, facilitating the development and the maintenance of a culture immersed in structural, human, political and symbolic elements, changing the school into one of achievement and success. In the seemingly intractable conditions facing schools at the present time, a collaborative culture would appear to be critical in meeting the attendant challenges. Leithwood, Begley and Cousins (1992:129) observe:

> such a culture appears to be adaptive to increasingly prevalent conditions associated with calls for reform such as: new and more complex expectations for student outcomes; school-leaders able to provide instructional leadership; high expectations by the public for its schools and many associated external pressures or change; a rapidly expanding body of technical know-how concerning instruction; and changing family environments.

These are significant and pertinent findings and offer insights of value for this investigation. Whilst studies in the United States, Canada and Britain have been carried out to identify the nature of a collaborative culture, few address the notion of what it is that leaders actually *do* in schools to promote, develop and sustain a collaborative culture. Findings of the exploratory study and a review of the related theory and research suggested that the issue of collaborative leadership in schools is one of considerable professional interest and one worthy of further research. The research undertaken here thus attempts to broaden the existing knowledge in this domain. Chapter 3 which follows details the research methodology undertaken in this study, including the selection of schools, and data collection and analysis. It also addresses issues of validity and reliability and identifies the limitations of the study.

Chapter 3

Research Methodology

The theoretical discussion documented in the previous chapter paves the way for exploration of the key issues of this book, namely, what it is that leaders do to promote and develop collaborative cultures in their schools, and, how this collaborative leadership actually brings about success. That is what happens for students, teachers, and the organization as a whole, as a result of effective leadership? Answers to these questions were sought by interviewing a representative sample of 40 school leaders from five inner city schools in Melbourne, Australia. The process undertaken in reaching answers is detailed in this chapter.

Selection of Schools*

Five urban schools were identified and agreed to take part in the research for this book. They are as follows:

- Clematis Secondary College
- Kennedia Primary School
- Cassinia Secondary College
- Boronia West High School
- Banksia Primary School

The schools were either nominated or self-nominated and offered a mix of primary and secondary levels of schooling, as well as a range of characteristics associated with urban schools. Appendix 1 is an example of the profile questionnaire that was given to each of the participating schools.

Nominated schools were put forward by the manager of the Inner Melbourne Support Centre, in consultation with his staff, on the basis of their knowledge of the schools. Only one of the nominated schools, the Boronia West High School, took up the offer to participate in the book. The remainder of the

---

* Please note that all names of schools used here are fictitous and any resemblance is purely coincidental.

schools taking part were self-nominated. The opportunity to self-nominate arose as a result of a meeting held for urban school principals, where the book was outlined and principals were briefed as to the four criteria of success which the book was to address:

- Outstanding improvements in outcomes in recent years, in the program of the school as a whole or in one or more aspects of the program;
- Success in the introduction of new approaches to learning and teaching, or the organization or support of learning and teaching;
- Success in addressing a particular problem or set of problems;
- Sustained achievement over many years.

The principals offered to participate in the project if they felt their school met the criteria for success. Kennedia Primary School, Clematis Secondary College, Cassinia Secondary School and Banksia Primary School nominated themselves and thus became part of the project. Five schools in total, therefore, became part of the investigation, one nominated and four self-nominated.

The *Boronia West High School* was nominated by the Manager of the Inner Melbourne Support Centre, in consultation with his staff, on the basis of sustained achievement over many years, and continued success in the introduction of new approaches to learning and teaching, particularly in catering for children who may not have found success in more traditional settings.

Clematis Secondary College nominated itself for its success in addressing a particular problem, namely 'responding to its community and accommodating its educational needs' resulting in outstanding improvements in outcomes in recent years in the program of the school as a whole. This is evident in the elective system of subjects designed 'to provide students with a greater sense of empowerment over their school lives, and a greater commitment to their studies by putting the greatest degree of choice about subjects studied in the hands of students and their families.' This has been achieved by the introduction of a vertical structure for both academic and pastoral domains, that accommodates the needs of a school community with 'a trait of Mediterranean and Asian cultures for a strong emphasis on the family, with other siblings looking after younger ones.'

Kennedia Primary School sees its success lying in the organization and support of teaching and learning where 'all members of a diverse school community work harmoniously together, with multicultural teacher aides providing valuable liaison between home, school and the broader community'; where a tradition of democratic decision-making exists, the school council is functioning effectively and the degree of parental support and interest in educational issues is increasing; where all staff are involved in the school's committee structure; where staff members are co-operative and supportive of each other; where there is on-going professional development; where there is a commitment to social justice issues and, where policy-writing, evaluation and review of curriculum development are established components of school organization and are working effectively. In addition, there has been innovation in the curriculum, namely a comprehensive Personal Development program and a Visual Arts program and the development of the Maths Task Centre.

Cassinia Secondary College identified outstanding improvements in outcomes in recent years, in one or more aspects of the school program, as the reason for their inclusion in the project. They describe their accomplishments as the introduction of a comprehensive Year 9/10 elective program, which allows 'some choice and some specialization, but maintains breadth and allows Frameworks Units (areas of disciplined study) to be tailored to the local area or changing circumstances or student interests'; the full integration of technology into the year 7–10 program; the provision of a Technology Program for local primary schools; a strong Transition Program in partnership with local primary schools; the formation of the Cassinia Yarra Schools Group; well-developed student welfare and Integration initiatives; a comprehensive Careers/Counselling program; and An Equal Opportunity Program to enhance the position of minority groups, including girls.

Banksia Primary School believes its success is centred around the introduction of new approaches to the organization and support of learning and teaching. It cites 'great policies, cooperation, team efforts at all levels, open decision-making, promotion of people who are doing well, and involvement in the local community' as inclusive of its accomplishments.

These five urban schools, their staff, their students and their parents, provided the context for this research and the source of its findings. Not all schools were fully collaborative in all aspects. The findings have been drawn from those areas where the majority of participating schools were collaborative. It is not to be implied, therefore, that all findings necessarily apply to all schools. Whilst for the purposes of analysis, findings have been separated into the structural, human resource, political and symbolic frames, it is acknowledged that these four aspects are inextricably interrelated, and are simultaneously interwoven in practice.

Data Collection and Analysis

I used a qualitative approach as an appropriate means of investigating the research questions in order to provide rich descriptions and explanations of situational influences. This is a conscious move away from the positivist, reductionist approach of behaviourism to a more descriptive, naturalistic phenomenology of leaders in action. Qualitative research 'assumes that systematic inquiry must occur in a natural setting rather than an artificially constrained one such as an experiment' (Marshall and Rossman, 1989:10). Its purpose is to work from the setting in which the inquiry is being made so that the depth of complexities surrounding the topic of the book can be uncovered and linked appropriately to the findings; that is, a holistic understanding can be gained. Qualitative research methodology also allows for insight from the subject's view of what is being studied, not simply from the author's. This brings authenticity, as well as the possibility of broadening the hypothesized parameters. The 'naturalistic' element (Crowther and Gibson, 1990; Stake, 1967) which exists in qualitative analysis helps the author go beyond initial preconceptions, allowing new realities for book to emerge.

At the outset of the investigation, preliminary data were gathered through the School Profile (Appendix 1) information about the history and community of the school, enrolment patterns, past events and achievements recent and future changes and areas of accomplishment for which the school was nominated.

The main body of data were collected through interview, observation and examination of documents, and analysed adopting the qualitative approach described by Miles and Huberman (1984:21ff) incorporating 'data reduction', 'data display' and 'conclusions: drawing/verifying'. This cyclical, interactive process, is represented in Figure 4 below. The three components of data analysis—data collection, data reduction and data display were interwoven in an ongoing data analysis process which operated throughout the life of the book.

Figure 4: *Components of data analysis: Interactive model*

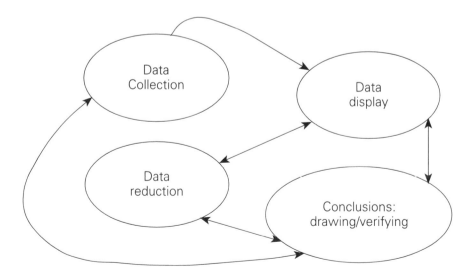

Data Collection

I adopted semi-structured data collection methods in preparing this book. This method supports the approach that it is both possible and desirable to employ a 'set of valid and verifiable *methods* for capturing these social relationships and their causes' (Miles and Huberman, 1984:20). I used predesigned interview questions with school leaders and a range of staff and members of the school community (Appendix 2). The way in which these questions were arrived at, and the thinking behind them, is illustrated in the following example taken from the symbolic frame:

- Collaborative leadership = structural + human resource + political + symbolic frames;
- Focus of question: symbolic leadership;
- Area for investigation: symbolic elements of collaborative leadership, and school success;
- Elements: beliefs
                              values
                              attitudes
                              norms of behaviour
                              symbols
                              rituals
                              ceremonies;
- Leader behaviour: to be identified in the book;
- School success   see p. 41

Elements for each frame (p. 23ff) were identified from the review of related literature. Questions of specific relevance to each frame have been drawn. Thus the questions for the symbolic frame became:

- What *shared* values run through the daily activities of school life?
- What do you and other leaders do to preserve and promote those values – in traditions and symbols of the school, or, informally?
- How has this brought about the successes achieved in the school – in terms of developing a sense of community, or having the collective confidence to manage the challenges faced by urban schools?
- Other?

Each set of questions was linked to collaborative leadership and school success. However, the focus changed according to which frame (structural, human resource, political or symbolic) was being addressed. This clearly delineated the area of investigation and tied the questions to the nature and purpose of the book, namely to investigate what leaders do to establish collaborative cultures in schools to bring about school success. The questions which have been drawn from the above process elicited:

a) responses which tapped into the symbolic elements present in the school;

b) information about what it was that leaders did in order to promote such a context;
c) how this has led to school success.

It is noted that questions needed modification, not in their content, but in terms of their language, to make them more user-friendly. Note was taken of the language style employed by the subjects and this was accommodated into the questioning.

All questions were developed using this process, with each of the four frames being addressed (see Appendix 2). A limit of three questions per frame was set, totalling twelve questions in all. This allowed subjects to raise additional, related factors which they saw as important and which I may have overlooked.

As well as interviews and open discussion, I examined extracts from documents and records and made observations. Predesigned questions delineated the area of book and kept me and the subjects focused, eliciting information pertinent to the study. This was necessary as the context of the book was relatively confined (to that of collaborative cultures and what leaders do to bring them about). I encouraged open discussion at the time of interview, during and following the predesigned questions and in other informal settings, allowing subjects to introduce new facets, not anticipated by me. This proved valuable, as often participants spoke freely and uninhibitedly once the tape recorder was turned off and when they knew their formal time frame had elapsed. I held eight one-hour, on-site interviews at each school in the following sequence: In a preliminary meeting with the principal, and others invited by the principal, I described in detail the nature of the book and how I would seek information about the school and its achievements, so that a profile of the school could be established in readiness for the main interviewing. A School Profile Questionnaire (Appendix 1) was distributed to principals at this meeting to be completed and returned prior to the initial school meetings. Information gathered from the School Profile Questionnaire provided important advance background material about the selected schools, such as the nature of the school's achievements, a general description of how leadership was exercised in the school, and its history and community, allowing the valuable face-to-face interview time to be spent on investigating pertinent issues relevant to collaborative leadership. It also provided a useful starting point on which to base specific questions for the structured interview questions.

The first interview at each school was held with the principal. As with other interview subjects, I sought a general account of causal linkages between the elements of collaborative leadership and school success. This meeting provided further opportunities for identification of other leaders, formal or informal, present in the school community who might give vital input. I also requested interviews with a selection of staff *not* seen formally as leaders, who represented the view of the 'teacher-at-large'. The latter provided a balance of views and an independent source of information.

The identified leaders were usually interviewed on a one-to-one basis. However, on three occasions interviews took place in small groups. Overall, forty interviews were undertaken, approximately eight in each of the five schools. Interviewees were a mix of teachers, students and parents, all seen as leaders of their school communities.

I held a final meeting, after initial data analysis had been completed, with the principal to discuss the key points and close the gaps, and requested further documentation as appropriate. Observation was interwoven throughout with school visits and supplemented with verbal and written material.

Table 1: Number of People Interviewed

School	Principal	Teachers/Aides	Parents	Students	Total
Clematis Secondary	1	7	1	–	9
Kennedia Primary	1	5	1	3	10
Cassinia Secondary	1	7	–	1	9
Boronia West High School	1	3	1	3	8
Banksia Primary	1	5	1	3	10
Total	5	27	4	10	46

Data Reduction

Each interview was taped, and with the subject's approval, transcripts were made, together with any additional comments made after taping had ceased. Immediately after each interview the key points that emerged were listed (for example, 'striving for consensus', 'interpersonal openness', 'shared beliefs'). Later these elements were classified and categorized into the four frames – structural, human resource, political and symbolic, first subject-by-subject, and then school-by-school. I noted elements of related leader behaviour and identified student, teacher and organizational outcomes. Data from the five schools were cross referenced and cross-site analysis was undertaken. These data were revisited many times, being sifted and resifted, classified and reclassified, summarized and resummarized until eventually refined to a distilled form where the findings presented themselves accurately and cogently. Figure 4 (p. 31) above illustrates the approach. Finally hypothesized causal links were drawn between leadership behaviour and school success in terms of student, teacher and organizational outcomes.

Data Display

I recorded findings in two distinct formats, in each of the four frames. First, in an extended narrative mode using the descriptions gathered from interviews and documentation to exemplify specific outcomes. Second, in a list format which gave concise findings summarizing:

- the behaviour exhibited by leaders in the schools, that is, what they actually do to promote, develop and sustain a collaborative culture in their schools;
- how collaborative leadership has achieved success in the five project schools;
- hypothesized causal linkages between the findings of each frame and school success – student, teacher and organizational outcomes.

These two forms of data display complement each other, in that the former provides a descriptive, naturalistic account of leaders in action, whereas the latter acknowledges that those interested in the book, including members of the participating schools, desire results and recommendations disseminated effectively and efficiently, in a form that is succinct and facilitates use; one from which conclusions can be drawn and, importantly, action taken. As Morris, *et al.* (1987) state 'give the audience what it needs to know – and no more . . . present an evocative report that matches the style of the audience.' Causal relationships, depicting the precise linkages and interactive pathways between the elements of collaboration and the elements of success, supplement the narrative mode of the report and parallels work by other authors in the leadership domain (see particularly Leithwood and Jantzi, 1990; Miles, 1987). The combination of these two forms of display offers an organized body of information from which conclusions can be drawn and, importantly, action taken.

Validity and Reliability

Conclusions were drawn inductively using the process outlined above. The validity and reliability of this conclusion-drawing needs to be established. Consequently, worked through examples of precisely how findings were reached from the primary data, and how causal links were hypothesized from the findings, have been presented in Chapters 5, 6, 7 and 8 where the findings and the hypothesized causal links of each frame have been reported.

Critics of early qualitative approaches argued that imprecise measurement, weak generalizability of findings, vulnerability to bias, overload of data and extreme labour intensiveness make qualitative methods less than desirable. Over the last decade, greater sophistication has been devised in naturalistic methodology (Crowther and Gibson, 1990:40; Miles and Huberman, 1984). Nonetheless, it is important to keep the critics' concerns to the fore to ensure that a qualitative book does not veer away from a research project and enter instead the realms of a good story. 'The meanings emerging from the data have to be *tested* for their plausibility, their sturdiness, their "confirmability" –that is their *validity*' (Miles and Huberman, 1984:22). The conceptual framework used in this book alleviates many of the misgivings held by antagonists of qualitative research and accords such validity. It provides a legitimate means of guiding the research design so that data can be satisfactorily organized and analysed, increases the opportunity for significant findings to emerge, simplifies the complex task of interpreting results, and assures research is cumulative from one book to the next. Hocking and Caldwell (1990:7) explain:

> It [the conceptual framework] provides a means of focussing and, to some degree, bounding the collection of data. It facilitates the clarification of research questions and sources of data. The framework ensures comparability in multi-site case studies and forms the basis for subsequent data reduction. Finally the conceptual framework provides the logic for organising the analysis of data. It should be noted, however, that the conceptual framework should not limit the introduction of new elements which may emerge in the course of data collection, nor constrain the interpretation of the significance of, or relationship between, the various elements.

The nature of qualitative analysis leaves it open to subjective bias. Naturalistic inquiry is an intensely personal process and 'the unknowing author can colour, taint or distort both the process itself and eventual research outcomes through the intrusion of personal values, attitudes and biases' (Crowther and Gibson, 1990:41). Personal biases must, therefore, be declared. At this point it is necessary to acknowledge that my professional position is one that supports collaboration in school processes and activities. Further the preferred mode of operating in a collaborative context is through the symbolic frame. This personal stance has been taken into account during the research process so that these predispositions can become a research asset rather than a research liability:

> while the subjective role of the author is a critical variable in the qualitative research process, there is no compelling reason to regard it as a problem of consequence. Quite the contrary: once it is realised that one's subjectivity can be understood, it becomes obvious that it can be a valuable ally. The potential rewards would seem to be extremely worthwhile – research that itself is more exciting and meaningful, personal investigative capabilities that are more sensitive and enriched understandings of one's own values and feelings (Crowther and Gibson, 1990:46).

Keeping issues of validity and author subjectivity clearly in mind, a concerted attempt was made to conform to the characteristics of the *ideal* author (author's emphasis) described by Miles and Huberman (1984:46):

- some familiarity with the phenomenon and the setting under book;
- strong conceptual interests;
- a multi-disciplinary approach, as opposed to narrow grounding or focus in a single discipline;

- good 'investigative' skills, including doggedness, the ability to draw people out, and the ability to ward off premature closure.

In this way it was possible to adhere to a clear focus, encourage the emergence of all relevant information, produce clear, verifiable and replaceable findings, and avoid data overload and undue labour-intensiveness.

Limitations of the Study

This study analysed findings from five urban schools. It is acknowledged that these do not represent a sample of *outstanding* urban schools and that findings cannot be generalized across urban schools *per se*. The research focused on what leaders *do* in schools to create the conditions for the collaborative cultures which, in turn, create success in schools. The intention of the study is to illuminate good practice, in an area not previously addressed, in the five selected schools. It does not lay claim to being representative of other schools in Australia, though findings could be generalized to other similar urban schools in Melbourne. It is likely that a wider study, with carefully chosen samples of urban schools and whose success is defined more precisely, will furnish findings which can be applied across urban schools in general.

Reflections on the Methodology

The Qualitative Approach

A qualitative methodological approach proved to be entirely adequate for this research project. In particular the interview component, which though time consuming for both interviewer and interviewees, achieved its objective of providing rich and insightful information in response to the research questions. The inclusion of open-ended questions, inviting comment on relevant factors which did not arise from responses to the predesigned interview questions, was helpful in establishing the complete picture. Interviews reaped a wealth of data which may not have been tapped via single questionnaire or survey methods. Taping of the interviews proved invaluable. It allowed for greater personal interaction with the interview subject during the interviews themselves, freeing me from note-taking and consequent diversion from interpersonal exchange. Visits to schools established a personal connection with those taking part in the book encouraging expansive responses. A number of interviewees commented on the strength of the discussion which emanated from the interview process, and its superiority to written responses which in their view are impersonal in nature and often completed in haste. School visits provided the opportunity to observe the school at work. Additional documentation, such as policy statements, were useful in supplementing interview responses and providing detail. The School Profile Questionnaire (Appendix 1) initiated a bank of information about the participating schools prior to the interview process, establishing a large volume of preliminary data as a spring-board to the ensuing investigation. The combination of interview responses, the School Profile, extracts from school documentation and observation proved to be an effective data base from which to draw findings. In my view the validity and the reliability of the findings were enhanced as a result of the methodology undertaken and encourages others to adopt its use in any naturalistic inquiry.

The process of data reduction was exhaustive, allowing for constant re-definition of each of the collaborative elements across the four frames until a convincing accuracy developed. Miles and Huberman's (1984:23) interactive model worked well, capturing the interrelationships and cross connections between the components of data collection, data reduction, data display and conclusion drawing/verifying. The model also took account of the ongoing nature of the data analysis process, identifying the realities of the naturalistic research context which required repeated classifying and re-classifying of data. I recommend the use of the Miles and Huberman interactive model for those undertaking qualitative research.

Conceptual Issues

The conceptual framework served the needs of the investigation well. Taking time at the outset to carefully think through and design the conceptual frame-work in detail paid dividends in terms of its clarity and focus in developing the research questions. Consequently, the research questions returned responses with strong conceptual relevance. Extensive reading of the current literature and related research was a critical prerequisite to developing the conceptual framework. It was necessary to reach a point of convergence in the literature in order to move from transformational leadership in general to collaboration in particular, before any real inroads into the conceptual framework could be made. Of particular influence in this regard was the work of Fullan and Hargreaves (1991b); Leithwood and Jantzi (1990); Nias, Southworth and Yeomans (1989); and Rosenholtz (1989).

The design of the conceptual framework was effective in enabling the book of leadership behaviour, built up around the elements of collaboration, to be undertaken and to draw connections between collaboration and success. The Bolman and Deal (1991) frames proved helpful, providing a firm foundation from which to interpret and analyse the emerging collaborative elements. The four categories of structural, human, political and symbolic leadership embraced the complexity of the leadership milieu so that no blind spots could occur. Bolman and Deal's typology was highly applicable to the school context. However, I have one small comment to make regarding the symbolic frame. This frame was by far the most difficult to use as a basis for interpretation and analysis of data. Of course, the very nature of the symbolic elements makes this a difficult exercise. However, I found it necessary to draw on the work of Nias, Southworth and Yeomans (1989:11) to extricate a manageable structure for interpretation of the primary data within the symbolic frame. This structure was developed around beliefs, values, attitudes and norms of behaviour; symbols, rituals and ceremonies, and was found to be a indispensable additional mini-conceptual framework within the symbolic frame, providing a means to analyse and interpret the more complex data involved. An interesting observation was that other elements such as 'culture-founders' and 'culture-bearers', 'heroes' and 'cabals' espoused in the literature were not directly identified in this book. Any relationship of these in the findings was obtuse. Perhaps in the Australian school context the style of language used to describe such people would seem to be inappropriate and not part of the vernacular; or perhaps in the egalitarian culture of our society, people who work closely together do not conceive of each other in those terms. Whatever the case, they did not present in the findings of this book.

The intention of the book was to *illuminate* good practice, in an area not previously addressed, in the five selected schools. As discussed earlier, it does not lay claim to being representative of other schools in Australia, though findings could be generalizable to similar urban schools in Melbourne. However, I take the view that practitioner reflection on the good practices of the leaders in the successful schools of this investigation could bring insights to bear relevant to leadership in schools in general, and to leadership in urban schools in particular. This is particularly relevant in the stormy times that are facing Victorian schools at present. With widespread reorganization of roles and relationships at both the school and system levels, and variations in government policies and procedures made almost on a daily basis, creative leadership is imperative.

The focal issue still remaining to be explored is how the principal and other leaders in the school operated effectively in their schools? What, specifically was their role, and what did they actually do to achieve success? How do they use structural, human, political and symbolic elements to bring about positive student, teacher and organizational outcomes? How did structural, human resource, political and symbolic perspectives come into play? The research questions below were designed to gain answers to these issues.

What is it that leaders do to promote, develop and sustain collaborative cultures in schools?

How does collaborative leadership effect success in these schools?

The research questions were transposed into twelve Interview Questions (see Appendix 2). The four subsequent chapters give the responses to these questions. Forty-six interviews were held at the five participating schools. Those interviewed included principals, teachers, teacher aides, parents and students (see Table 1). The italicized text is a direct quotation of their replies. These explanations give powerful insights into the specifics of collaborative leadership as they play out in each of the four frames. Each chapter looks at one frame in turn, beginning with a structural perspective.

Chapter 4

The Structural Frame

Leaders in schools need to focus on structural arrangements if they are to transform their school into one of success. Structures in schools provide the means by which decisions are made and implemented; where goals are set, where planning is designed and carried out, where job descriptions are clarified, where roles are identified and responsibilities allocated. The structural frame aligns with Sergiovanni's (1984:6) concept of a 'technical force of leadership', where accomplishing the administrative tasks of the organization (planning, organizing, coordinating and controlling) are the central focus. Pertinent to this discussion are the external controls placed on Victorian schools directed by government-imposed school reform. In 1985 the Victorian Government deliberately departed from a tradition of centralized policy control, giving increased responsibilities for educational policies and planning to the schools themselves via their School Councils. Schools were to become 'self-managing' (Caldwell and Spinks, 1992:4), and 'to enable the school-based policy development process to be democratic, the legislation [provided] for council membership to be shared among the elected representatives of the chief interest groups namely, parents, teachers and, where appropriate, students' (Ministry of Education, Ministerial Paper Number 4:4.5). Subsequent to the writing of this book, further changes have been made in government policy and the above arrangements have been revised.

All the participating schools in this investigation functioned at the time through the formal structure of the overriding statutory body, the School Council, which took full responsibility for formulating policy, participating in the selection of the Principal and Deputy Principal, oversight of buildings and grounds, financial management and parent and community relations. Other formal bodies in the schools included the Administrative Committee, Curriculum Committees, the Students' Representative Council and various sub-committees such as Equal Opportunity and Parental Involvement. Participating schools managed their school planning, policy-making and organization via these bodies. Boronia West High School, as a small school, rarely worked through sub-committees in its decision-making processes, but operated as a whole staff in conjunction with its School Council and the Students' Representative Council. However, the process in all schools, directed by Ministry of Education guidelines, was that all school policy and overriding management issues recommended by teachers, students or parents went to School Council for consideration. Only when ratified by School Council could recommendations be adopted. It is against this background that collaboration between the various members of the school community took place.

Understandings gained from the related theory and research demonstrate that structural perspectives in a collaborative culture are inclusive of the following elements:

- democratic processes
- leadership density
- direction/vision
- shared goals
- shared responsibility
- roles
- coordination/planning
- respect and valuing of all
- listening
- frank, open and frequent communication

Keeping these elements clearly in mind, three of the twelve interview questions (Appendix 2) were directed at gaining insight into the way in which structural arrangements were organized in the schools, and how leaders[1] achieved success through these. The questions for the structural frame were:

- How is the school organized to allow shared decision-making and shared responsibility?
- What is it that you and other leaders actively do to promote these arrangements?
- How does this contribute to your school's success, for instance, in terms of more effective planning and coordination or clearer description of roles?
- Other?

These interview questions were developed from the conceptual framework (Chapter 3) to elicit specific data about the structural elements of collaborative leadership and how it brings about success in the five Melbourne urban schools under study.

Leadership and the Structural Frame

The overriding feature of leader behaviour in the participating schools was the strong commitment to, and belief in, the participatory democratic decision-making process. Officially the democratic structure was imposed by Ministry of Education directives outlined above, and its application in practice by leaders in these schools took on larger than life proportions and a vigilance to its principles which went far beyond routine procedures. '*Democracy matters*', were the words of the Staff Development Coordinator at Clematis Secondary.

Consultation and representation were the keystones of their operation, reflecting a valuing of others in the broad school community of staff, parents and students. This attitude seemed in turn to have the effect of bringing about reciprocal respect, support and a desire to give an active commitment to the organization from the whole school community. It appears that an atmosphere of respect and valuing of all members of the school community is generated when there is genuine professional regard for the abilities and input of those in leadership positions, be it the principal, teachers, parents or students. Age and experience are not necessarily contributing factors. Leaders took action to put procedures into place which ensured all people in their school were given openings to fully participate in the decision-making processes. This action centres around what Sergiovanni (1987:122) refers to as 'leadership density' where 'leadership roles are shared' and in which 'leadership is broadly exercised' amongst a broad range of teachers, whether senior or not, ancillary staff such as multicultural aides, students and parents.

At Cassinia Secondary College, '*Anyone who wants to can be part of any group, but people feel more like participating if they have a formal role*', commented one staff member. Seniority does not dictate the allocation of roles and responsibilities in most of the participating schools. At Clematis Secondary all jobs, except those of the principal and deputy principal, are open to everyone, and everyone is encouraged to apply (associated with this is the expectation that people do not hold on to the one position for an extended time giving as many people as possible the chance to be involved). Some positions are appointed (principal and deputy principal), some are elected (faculties vote for their coordinators); for others, a priority list of available positions is displayed and any teacher is able to indicate an interest. If there is more than one applicant for the position then the Administrative Committee conducts interviews and selects the best candidate for the job. Monetary allowances, normally allocated to senior positions of responsibility, are granted in order of prioritized positions *producing good people doing the job*. A senior member of staff at Clematis Secondary commended this approach:

> *In the old style administration people of talent and ability were being passed over . . . and people started to say 'let's do it [the selection of senior positions] another way' . . . people were very anguished over the idea that senior teachers and principals shouldn't have powers by right; that they should earn those powers and exercize those powers in the name of the people that they were working with.*

As far as the day-to-day running of the school is concerned the present principal of Clematis Secondary believes it is '*one of the most deeply democratically run schools that exist.*' Democratic procedures have been in existence since 1978. Since that time staff have had a significant say in whole school planning, as the staff development officer notes:

> *The nerve centre of the school is the staff meeting held once a week . . . it is recognized as* the *decision-making body of the school. This*

> *[democratic process] makes the chain of command very clear, so that if you want to know something, you know who to go to, and if you think something is not being done right or there's a problem, there's a very clear and commonly accepted way of bringing it to the surface and finding out what's wrong and fixing it, which doesn't in any sense depend on personalities.*

This approach leads to strong communication and clear structural processes for operational procedures. In addition, people at any level are empowered to make change.

The deputy principal at Clematis Secondary elaborates:

> *People know where the decisions will be made. They know, if something's happening that they don't like, where to go and to do something about it. People do feel that sort of ownership of the decisions – they mightn't like it but they do know that if you want to have a say then the price you pay for that, is that things are going to be decided that you might not like. It's a two-way street in that respect. That structure is very clear and it works well.*

Ultimately principals do have the right of veto, but in most cases its use was rare and was justified to staff. It is significant to note that overuse of the power of veto caused staff frustration, was counterproductive and an obstacle to success.

The importance to staff having a significant say in the organization of the school, and in their professional lives, is expressed by the student welfare teacher at Clematis Secondary:

> *In previous schools I was at, where places were run along very authoritarian lines with power structures lying in the hands of the principal and the deputy principal and one or two senior teachers, I was constantly in conflict. This hasn't been the case here and it's because of the fact that the structure set-up means that the people who you are responsible to here, given the guidelines given by the Education Department and the School Council role in the power structure in the school, are your peers. Now based on that, if I get a rejection on an idea or something that I put forward, I've got no fallback. It's been rejected by my peers. I think that's who should judge and determine whether ideas for the school on a whole range of areas, not just curriculum, should be based. Therefore I think the structures that are set up here are excellent in that way.*

Interconnections with the political frame are strong here. The democratic process means empowerment of others to make crucial decisions within the school. Leaders need to have trust and confidence in the process for it to work effectively.

Strongly correlated to the above is the active instigation by school leaders of democratic processes at the meeting level. Democratic procedures such as open meetings, rotating the Chair and minute-taking at meetings, and having an open agenda extend leadership opportunities and share responsibility across the staff and school community. Published outcomes of policies and minutes of meetings give everyone the opportunity to keep in touch with what is happening, particularly in large schools where it is physically impossible for all staff to attend all meetings. Having this information is seen as critical:

> *Information is the most important thing and information at this school is available to everybody. At every meeting that takes place minutes are taken and stored publicly. Everybody's timetable, everyone's allot-ment, is displayed on the noticeboards for everyone to read. There are no sweetheart deals, nobody can say this person's getting favours that we don't know about, because it's all public. Nobody gets any favours or expects them. It's extremely important that people don't feel there are any special deals for people on the basis of friendship or seniority; and it's also important so that people understand the methods that are used to administrate the place. If people want to make changes that sort of information is essential because you can't propose a change unless you know how the current system is operating* (Daily Organizer, Clematis Secondary College).

It seems that if democratic structures are in place and fair and equitable mechanisms are employed to reach decisions, people are able to accept and cooperate with those decisions even if they run counter to their particular preference.

In some schools formal meeting procedures are the routine practice and staff have required support to feel conversant or confident in dealing with the formalities, such as procedural motions/referral/gag/points of order. Leaders have put strategies into place where whole staff groups have broken up into small groups to encourage those who may be intimidated by the formalities and/or the experienced players of the large group, to feel comfortable in taking an active part. A secondary teacher reflects:

> *People need confidence and experience to work in the political sys-tem; in smaller groups they are more likely to have a say . . . teachers are reluctant to stand up and have a say . . . funny for teachers isn't it?*

Lack of confidence in coping with formal meeting procedures may not be the only obstacle to the successful implementation of democratic processes in schools. To return to Little's (1982a) significant finding, collaboration in schools is a rare occurrence, even though mandated at a government level here in Victoria. Barth (1990:129) suggests that reasons of self-interest may play a part in why this is so:

> When others are making the decisions, teachers can resist, lobby, hold out, attempt to influence a situation to their own advantage. When teachers work for the common good, they give up a large measure of

self-interest in the outcome. With leadership and responsibility comes the need to see others' points of view and act fairly in their eyes. Many teachers are not willing to make this trade.

As well as setting up formal democratic procedures leaders in the project schools initiated strategies to facilitate a welcoming and supportive atmosphere for parents. A parent representative of one School Council commented:

As a parent I see the organization in the sense that it is an open school, that we are welcome at any time . . . you don't feel that if there is a problem you can't go in . . . so there's an openness, there's a sense of belonging that's built up that this is our school, this is our community.

Some teachers endorse the Ministry's view of seeing parent participation as a philosophical necessity:

With the whole change of philosophy of education, that parents realize now that they have a right to be involved. When I first started teaching in the early 70s it was the reverse really, parents were really just struggling to get involved. I think with that sort of revolution, that responsibility has come with it and parents want to follow it through. I think teachers now realize, some more reluctantly than others, the benefits of sharing that educational responsibility. There are incredible benefits – the whole resource area of varied people, and (speaking as a parent myself) I know that I have got a lot to offer. Many parents can add through their involvement and make their children feel more comfortable – it's not just a sharp division between home and school. If we're talking about integrated education then there should never be a division, it should all just merge. I am very much against that very structured, closed view of institutionalized education . . . The principal is a strong advocate. It's clearly through all our policy statements that parents are invited to contribute and be involved.

Other teachers are not so sure. A dilemma can present itself for staff, for instance, in terms of implementation of curriculum policy which has been decided at the School Council level and with which teachers may not necessarily agree. Given the scenario where parents can have a very influential say, and through strength of personality, dominate the decision-making process, staff can feel very threatened, as one young primary teacher in this study asserts:

These people [ill-informed parents] are on my Council! These people are making decisions as to when I have my curriculum meetings, as to when I have my reports and what is to be part of my curriculum; these are the people who are ratifying my policy about how I should teach mathematics!

One view of addressing this is expressed below in the Sanderson High School's Case Book in Effective Schooling (1988:14). Sanderson High is a secondary school located in the Northern Territory of Australia:

> While increasing the level of parent and student input is actively encouraged, the main focus in decision-making at Sanderson High School continues to be the role of the teacher. Decision-making at Sanderson is designed to develop ownership of policy by those who are expected to implement it, namely the staff.

Employing inclusive strategies such as a round table arrangement, keeping meetings short and avoiding technical language encouraged greater parent participation in meetings at Banksia Primary. The President of the School Council elaborates:

> *We've worked it so that we have changed from a formal structure to a round table format in the last two or three years. We still go through a formal agenda; the underlying thing at a School Council meeting would be to get through the agenda on time. We also have another structure where if anybody talks about anything like LOTE or uses a technical term without explaining it, they have to put 20¢ in the middle because we discovered that the use of technical language was daunting to parents. You could sit through meetings for the first twelve months and while you would understand, you would not understand the implications because all this Ministry jargon was being used. So to make the language and the reporting in such a way that everybody was included, we don't talk about etcetera without explaining.*

Nonetheless one of the obstacles faced by some urban schools is the difficulty of drawing more than a handful of parents into active involvement in decision-making despite their constitutional inclusion as legitimate members of policy groups in the school, and its accompanying power to participate in discussion and decisions on school aims and goals, policies (including curriculum), the budget and program evaluation. Factors attributed to non-participation include language difficulties with English as the second language for a majority of parents, a perceived fear of schools and a lack of understanding of educational activities based on their past experience (many parents have experienced primary education only), cultural differences about the role of parents and the constraints associated with two working parents or parents working night-shifts. Obviously representation is severely limited in these schools and, as a result, the teaching staff tends to dominate the policy-making. Despite this, some creative efforts have been initiated in an attempt to redress this situation. Kennedia Primary has capitalized on its school community's passion for food. The School Principal explains:

> *Last year we had about 130 parents up for our AGM, which is unbelievable, because at all our community involvement things we*

encourage food. We ask parents to bring a plate [of food]. It seems to encourage them a lot. Just to come up and hear the Head speak – we would get nobody. But with food! . . . and we've got our six ethnic teacher aides who will be there in attendance to interpret. Parents will support the school in things where they don't seem threatened, for instance, school concerts (the Town Hall was chockers – upstairs, downstairs, everywhere; they will support it no end), working bees, a multicultural night, even information nights – we have two a year on different curriculum areas. We get a huge turn up at that again, but, there's food involved each time.

Opportunities are offered for leadership across a broad spectrum of people within the school communities. Ethnic teacher aides play a vital role in this respect. Teacher aides in urban schools are critical to parent involvement as they provide the essential link between the school and the parent of non-English speaking families. At Kennedia Primary where, at last census only nine children in the school spoke English at home, teacher aides play a significant leadership role, actively encouraged by the principal and the School Council President. There is one program aide and five ethnic aides for Arabic, Vietnamese, Turkish, Portuguese and Greek. They work in classrooms alongside teachers, they organize drop-in times in the community room, talk with parents, communicate by telephone if the need arises, undertake home visits, act as parent liaison, attend school functions such as curriculum meetings, where they translate and interpret curriculum issues, and assist in translating all documentation so it can be understood by all. As well as translation and interpreting, the teacher aides play an important social role in making all groups feel welcome and at home, bringing everyone together and building a sense of school community. A multicultural aide at Kennedia Primary School explains: '*The social aspect is paramount. People who aren't comfortable with English don't want to sit and listen to a formal report-style meeting. We bring a plate of food, socialize and then casually get the message across.*'

Urban school leaders are also aware of the need to be attuned to the cultural politics of the ethnic groups in their school. It is imperative to success, for example, to select a suitable ethnic teacher aide. At Kennedia Primary, where parents are Christian Arabic, a *Christian* Arabic, not a *Muslim* Arabic, aide is essential. Clearly a cultural match is necessary. At Grevillea Primary School the reverse is necessary – a Muslim Arabic parent group demands a Muslim Arabic teacher aide. In addition, there is often a mix of cultures, and together with the transience of the parent populations, an astute principal is constantly monitoring any changes and planning for appropriate ethnic aide staffing as the need arises.

Whatever the approach, concerted attempts by leaders to include parents in the decisionmaking process appear to be essential if success is to be achieved. Susan Moore Johnson (1990:336) in her book on the American teacher's workplace strongly recommends that 'public schools must engage parents more meaningfully in the education of their children and coordinate public services on behalf of children and their families.'

Leaders take conscious steps to ensure that a breadth of leadership opportunities are offered to a range of people across the school community developing an understanding of the complexities of managing a school and bringing a democratic approach to the selection of positions of responsibility in the school. At Kennedia Primary the Principal commented:

> *Everyone, regardless if they're straight out of college, has extra responsibilities; it helps them to grow professionally because it makes them develop other skills. My job is to be able to judge a person and to give them a responsibility that they can do well.*

This approach mirrors Barth's (1990:128) comment:

> When teachers are enlisted and empowered as school leaders, everyone can win. Other teachers' concerns are frequently better understood by one of their fellows than by someone who performs a different job. Important schoolwide issues receive more care and attention when the adult is responsible for few other major areas. And the principal wins by recognizing that there is plenty of leadership to go round. If the principal tries to do all of it, much of it will be left undone by anyone. Leadership is not a zero–sum game in which some person gets some only when another loses some. In fact, the principal gains influence and demonstrates leadership by entrusting some of it to others. Being accorded leadership generates new leadership.

Undoubtedly there are strong connections here with the human resource frame with its focus on professional and personal needs and satisfaction. Effective leaders see the connections between leadership opportunity and professional development where, leadership density leads to professional development in a broad-ranging group of staff:

> *If someone's got the ability and a real desire to get up and take a program on, you don't want to say 'sorry you can't do it because senior people have that responsibility', so we try and weigh it up so that senior teachers are carrying their expected loads (because they've got the expertise hopefully), but if there is someone from within the school who has that expertise we open up those possibilities for them. Often, say, if there's an acting position of responsibility within the school, what we do is advertise the requirements and anybody in the school who feels they have something to bring to that position can apply. So it's not just on seniority . . . We have our criteria for selection and one of them, which I think is good, is that a professional development component is built in. That way we can rotate positions because part of someone's professional development is that they take*

> *on responsibility. Sometimes you can get locked into the position where,*
> *because you're senior, or because you've had that job for x-amount*
> *of years, it's considered yours. There's a sense of ownership. This way*
> *we can break out of that ownership criteria and go on the needs of*
> *the school and on the professional growth of the applicants (senior*
> *teacher, Banksia Primary School).*

Leaders in the project schools have a commitment to this belief and are pre-pared to accommodate the lengthier and more difficult process that is required when demarcation of roles is not clear and applicants' needs are taken into consideration. Leaders are wrestling with the practical application of the notion of leadership density. No one doubts its wisdom, but juggling all its associated demands is no easy task – rationality and structure are intertwined with equity, and the joint valuing of both experience and youth. However, it is clear that democratic procedures in school decision-making, open meetings, access to information and an open door policy to all members of the school community, contribute to school success.

Collaborative Leadership and School Success – Structural Frame

A significant belief for leaders in the project schools is the primary purpose these democratic processes serve. As a social justice issue democracy holds much sway, but, importantly, the overriding intention of participatory decision-making was to ensure that educational programs of the school met the needs of its students and, as a result, the educational agenda was advanced. So it was a compelling sense of direction for the school's fundamental mission, which was driving the daily work of all those in the school, with a sharp focus on learning and teaching and the needs of the students in their care. The demo-cratic processes were developed to expedite this purpose. Leaders in success-ful schools were able to develop a school climate which directly focused on the centrality of teaching and learning using the structural arrangements of the school to support and enhance individual student achievement. In the 1990 School Council Annual Report, Banksia Primary School, makes this clear in its opening words:

> Banksia Primary is deeply committed to identifying and responding to
> the educational needs of its students and the community it serves. It
> does this by maintaining an open-door policy, and encouraging and
> nurturing all avenues of communication, formal and informal.

This includes making the formal structures and processes work for students within the context of government policy as is illustrated in the curriculum section of the Banksia Primary 1990 Annual Report:

Through the 1989 school development plan, school policies were developed in the following areas: Language, Mathematics, Pupil Welfare, Computer Studies, Integration and Communication . . . These projects translate directly into the successful classroom programs that combine to form the basis of a very successful year for the students in our care.

In its response to the School Profile (Appendix 1) Banksia Primary School reported its school success as centred around the introduction to new approaches in the organization and support of learning and teaching, citing 'great policies, open decision-making, promotion of people who are doing well, and involvement in the local community' as inclusive of its achievements.

At Boronia West High School, in addition to a weekly administrative meeting, all teachers meet together once a fortnight to discuss students' social, emotional or academic needs. Meeting as one group keeps all staff informed of any special needs of a particular student and assists them in working together as a combined front in addressing them. As a result, '*we all know about all students in the school*', the coordinator explains. Student-focused staff meetings highlight individual needs of students, leading to innovative curriculum and the development of student learning. A former student of Boronia West High, and now a replacement teacher, comments:

> *To be a successful teacher in this school you have to have the respect of the kids . . . Definitely, if kids don't put their best foot forward, they're letting the side down, and the teachers who they respect and look up to . . . Kids respect the teachers here – very much so.*

The opportunity to confront philosophical issues was also provided by these meetings. Leaders who actively linked meetings to a student focus clearly brought direct benefits to children both in terms of a relevant curriculum catering to individual needs and in terms of individualized student pastoral care which encouraged positive student attitudes both to their learning and in their relationships with others. School success at Boronia West High hinged on these leadership strategies. This school was nominated on the basis of sustained achievement over many years and continued success in the introduction of new approaches to teaching and learning.

A Year 12 student at Boronia West High comments on the teaching and learning approach. '*It helps you to find out who you are as an individual . . . Students take responsibility for themselves in their self-development and their learning . . . staff are there to assist, not to control.*' Traditional secondary teaching methodologies do not suit the students at Boronia West High, as one Year 12 girl explains:

> *Because the classes are so small you can have really, really good class discussions which are often better than just a whole period of copying down what the teacher says. We've never done that before. We've never actually come into a class, sat down, and for the whole period*

> *copied down what the teacher's writing on the board. And the first time that happened to me was when I went to [school x] – biology. And the teacher for the whole class hardly said a word to us and just wrote and wrote and wrote, and we just copied, copied, copied. None of it sunk in – you're too busy, copying, watching the board . . . trying to keep up with him [the teacher]. Then he says, 'go through your notes again at home.'*

Cassinia Secondary College transformed several existing school pro-grammes, particularly at the Years 7 to 10 levels, to better serve the demands of its multicultural, non-English speaking, adolescent clientele; acknowledg-ing the need to target individual differences in student learning and offer greater subject choice. These programs have been developed in response to the needs of students in an urban context. Certainly it has taken the combined efforts of staff, coordinated through shared decision-making, that has enabled these developments to take place. Children benefit directly in ways that the cur-riculum coordinator at Cassinia Secondary College points out. *'There is more choice, which makes learning more interesting. The free market* [approach] *provides healthy competition. The more attractive the subjects, the more stu-dents will select them.'*

Clematis Secondary College showed an adeptness and expertise in using participatory decision making structures as a dependable means of reaching insightful resolutions to the demanding educational issues which perpetually arose. As a combined staff with a single-minded purpose, (and jointly sharing the responsibility for the achievement of that purpose). The principal of Clematis Secondary considers the matter of elective subjects and sees them as, *'a reflec-tion of the democratic processes, in that students, with their family, have a greater say in what their program will be . . . not – in Year 7 do this! They have a big say in what they want to do.'* It appears there are clear connections between the structural arrangements of this school, and the school's success. *'The structure assists people to feel comfortable in their commitment here.'* (principal, Clematis Secondary)

Kennedia Primary School attributes its success to the way in which all staff work cooperatively together through school structures and processes to de-velop and extend the educational environment of its students. Diversity in the student clientele abounds, both in terms of cultural background and socio-economic need. Staff have to be fully on task, jointly communicating, problem-solving, and putting students first and foremost at all times, to really make a difference to the educational present, and future, of their young students. This is achieved by an unerring commitment to democratic decision making and inclusiveness of the whole school community.

A long-serving staff member at Kennedia Primary, currently the Year 5/6 class teacher, comments on the success of the school in achieving harmony in a diverse school community with the aid of democratic decision-making. *'It's the happiest staff I've worked with. The processes have been followed and things have been discussed. Hierarchy doesn't exist. Pulling rank doesn't exist.* The president of the School Council at Kennedia Primary believes, '*There is a greater collective knowledge and community involvement at the school, which is good considering the 43% transiency* [of students].' Success has been achieved in drawing the multicultural groups together.

The structures in place in the schools contribute significantly to school success. Leaders in the project schools facilitated school success through careful organization of their school's management structures. This approach is consistent with Beare, Caldwell and Millikan's (1989:112) examination of leadership studies which 'demonstrate that outstanding schools provide strong support for school-based management and collaborative decision-making within a framework of state and local policies.' They are also indicative of collaborative planning and collegial relationships described by Purkey and Smith (1985:358) where 'the staff of each school is given a considerable amount of responsibility and authority in determining the exact means by which they address the problem of increasing academic performance.' Success for the schools in this project has been strengthened by the structural dimension of collaborative leadership.

Development of Findings

Findings were drawn from the whole body of data gathered from each of the forty-six interviewees, school documentation and observation. One school at a time was researched and, after an initial interview with the school principal, interviews were arranged to suit the school program. All subjects were asked the same questions, though the opportunity was given to talk freely around the questions in an extended sense, allowing the depth of complexities surrounding the topic to emerge. Each interview was taped, with one exception at the subject's request, and later transcribed in detail. Each transcript of each of the subjects' responses was analysed through the four frames by categorizing the interview responses into the structural, human resource, political and symbolic elements. Using Miles and Huberman's (1984) interactive model, findings from *each frame* were then generalized across each of the subjects from a particular school, for example, Banksia Primary School, then cross-referenced and analysed across the five participating schools. These data were revisited many times, being classified and reclassified until eventually the findings were refined to the distilled form presented below. Figure 4 (p. 31) illustrates the approach. What follows first however, are two worked-through examples of the way in which primary data were transposed into the succinct findings listed below. These examples come from the structural frame. Each finding was developed via the same process. This chapter reports the findings of the *structural* frame.

Example 1

Primary data

Extract from 1990 School Council Annual Report – Banksia Primary School:

Banksia Primary is deeply committed to identifying and responding to the educational needs of its students and the community it serves. It does this by maintaining an open-door policy and encouraging and nurturing all avenues of communication, formal and informal.

Interview response from staff development officer at Clematis Secondary College:

The nerve centre of the school is the staff meeting held once a week . . . it is recognized as the decision-making body of the school. This [democratic process] makes the chain of command very clear, so that if you want to know something, you know who to go to, and if you think something is not being done right or there's a problem, there's a very clear and commonly accepted way of bringing it to the surface and finding out what's wrong and fixing it, which doesn't in any sense depend on personalities.

Interview response from the deputy principal at Cassinia Secondary College:

every second Wednesday we meet to discuss areas of concern in working groups. It's an action process. We identify common areas of concern and common action.

The above primary data leads to the finding

Leaders in the project schools provide clearly communicated mechanisms/structures based on democratic principles for whole school planning.

Example 2

Primary data

Interview response from a senior staff member at Clematis Secondary College:

In the old style administration people of talent and ability were being passed over . . . and people started to say 'let's do it [the selection of senior positions] another way' . . . people were very anguished over the idea that senior teachers and principals shouldn't have powers by right; that they should earn those powers and exercise those powers in the name of the people that they were working with.

Interview response from preparatory teacher at Banksia Primary School:

> *With the whole change of philosophy of education, parents realise now that they have a right to be involved. When I first started teaching in the early 70s it was the reverse really. Parents were really just struggling to get involved. I think with that sort of revolution, that responsibility has come with it and parents want to follow it through. I think teachers now realize, some more reluctantly than others, the benefits of sharing that educational responsibility. There are incredible benefits – the whole resource area of varied people, and (speaking as a parent myself) I know that I have got a lot to offer. Many parents can add through their involvement and make their children feel more comfortable – it's not just a sharp division between home and school. If we're talking about integrated education then there should never be a division, it should all just merge. I am very much against that very structured, closed view of institutionalized education . . . The principal is a strong advocate. It's clearly through all our policy statements that parents are invited to contribute and be involved.*

Interview response from a Year 12 student at Boronia West High School:

> *This school is running because of us and we have to have a say in what's going on. It makes for less tension . . . you can do something about things; people listen to your point of view.*

The above primary data leads to the finding

> *Collaborative leaders support a participatory democratic process for selection of positions of responsibility which are shared across the staff, parents and students of the school.*

The preceding narrative reflects the pattern of responses which repeatedly emerged from the interviewees. Comments were unprompted and immediate, expressed with clarity and coherence. The consistency of responses over the nearly 40 hours of interviews leads to a certainty and confirmation of the following generalized findings.

Findings of the Structural Frame

What is it that leaders do to promote, develop and sustain collaborative cultures in urban schools?

Leaders in the project schools of this investigation facilitate:

- a school climate which directly focuses on the centrality of teaching and learning and can use the structural arrangements of the school to support and enhance individual student achievement;

- an open-door policy which invites and promotes all people to show expressions interest in school decision-making;
- a participatory democratic process for selection of positions of responsibility which are shared across the staff, parents and students of the school;
- clearly communicated mechanisms/structures, based on democratic principles, for whole school planning;
- democratic processes at the meeting level, ie., rotation of Chair and minute-taking;
- freely shared information to the whole school community;
- opportunities for all to take an active part in the formal processes of the school.

Characterized by:

- a central focus of using school structures to address and to support students' learning;
- commitment, belief and trust in the democratic process;
- the knowledge that decisions have been arrived at in a fair and equitable way;
- openness and a sense of belonging;
- respect and valuing of all members of the school community;
- a secure and relaxed atmosphere;
- an absence of structural hierarchy and autocratic decision-making;
- representation of all sectors of the school community;
- responsibility not purely linked to seniority;
- avoidance of ownership of positions of responsibility;
- encouragement of others to take on positions of responsibility, accompanied by strong informal and formal support;
- initiation of change from staff, student or parent-base rather than principal/executive administration.

How does collaborative leadership effect success in these schools?

It brings about:

- clear communication and guidelines;
- sound, effective and well-understood decisions;
- efficient operating of the school through effective planning;
- trust and confidence in the decision-making process;
- a sense of empowerment;
- a strongly committed staff;
- high teacher morale;
- high level of teacher involvement;
- a cohesive, supportive staff;
- maximum opportunities for input of staff, student and parent talent/skills; broad-ranging professional development;

- a shared workload;
- more harmonious relationships – staff/staff, staff/student, student/ student, staff/parent.

Summary and Conclusion

The structural frame emphasizes the importance of formal roles and relationships. The focus is on organizational direction and goals, roles, policies, procedures, and coordination and planning. In a collaborative environment there is a breadth of leadership, an absence of hierarchy and the opportunity for all school community members to contribute to and influence the decision-making of the school. Above all, elements of structural leadership such as democratic processes, leadership density, shared goals, shared responsibility, coordination/planning, frank and frequent communication, are an institutionalized part of the day-to-day operations of the school. Structures must serve processes which are seen to be equitable and fair. Leaders in the schools studied have made a shift away from hierarchically-ordered organizational management to a leadership with an emphasis on democratic procedures which are inclusive rather than exclusive, seeing the operation of the school as a collective responsibility of staff, parents and, where appropriate, students. Leaders who establish a collaborative culture through the perceptive management of the structural arrangements of their school play a significant part in contributing to their school's success.

Note

1 In reference to the usage of the term 'leader' it must be noted that all interview subjects quoted in this book, whatever their title (for example, class teachers, faculty heads, integration teacher) are defined as 'leaders'.

Chapter 5

The Human Resource Frame

The human resource perspective delineated in this book is built around the view that organizations are populated by individuals who have needs, feelings and prejudices. The particular emphasis of this book is one of *professional* needs, feelings and prejudices, combining what Sergiovanni (1984:6) would term human and educational perspectives. Human factors including consideration of relationships among people in the school, morale and empowerment, instructional leadership, developing and evaluating curriculum, and professional development. All these take into account the urgency for collaboration, rather than isolation in leadership, as discussed in Chapter 2.

Chapter 4 addressed the issue of what it is that leaders do, through the structural frame, in urban schools to develop a collaborative culture and to achieve success for students. This chapter looks at the same issues but instead with a human resource focus. Collaborative elements associated with effective human resource leadership are used as a base for analysing responses from the forty or so interviewees in the five urban schools participating in this project. The human resource elements are as follows:

- centrality of teaching and learning;
- strong sense of community;
- value and regard for professional development;
- teachers as curriculum leaders;
- parents as co-partners;
- teams;
- teachers teaching teachers;
- professional honesty and openness;
- support, praise and trust;
- acceptance;
- sharing;
- continuous learning;
- continuous improvement;
- positive student/staff relations;
- staff cohesion.

Specific interview questions were designed to elicit insights from the human resource frame as to exactly what leaders[1] did in their schools to develop a collaborative culture. They were three of a series presented to encompass the full range of leadership behaviour across the four frames (see Appendix 2). Questions were as follows:

- In what ways do staff and others support and cooperate with each other – in their teaching practice, or personally?
- What do you and other leaders do to foster such cooperation and support – formally and informally?
- How has this influenced school successes, say, in professional development, or curriculum innovation?
- Other?

Leadership and the Human Resource Frame

The human resource frame is built on the fundamental premise that the individual talents, skill and energy of the people in an organization are its most vital resource. There is a constant interplay between the individual and the organization to ensure a fit between administrative goals and goals of individual members. The human resource frame here is focusing on the social aspect of human behaviour where 'man is essentially [seen as] a social animal and gains his basic sense of identity from relationships with others' (Handy, 1985:32). If organizations are alienating in their operation, valuable human talents are lost and human lives become malnourished (Deal, 1990). Effective leadership acknowledges the fact that people and organizations need each other. Organizations need professional experience, ideas and commitment; people need satisfying work, an income, and social and personal expression. As one reflective primary teacher at Kennedia Primary School notes, *'People with a need to express themselves in the organization are kept happy – that has a positive effect on the organization; people's needs are met, they're happier in their workplace and that affects their teaching.'* Good leadership is sensitive to this interdependence, arranging structures and conditions to meet the professional and personal needs of staff. Clark and Meloy (1989:273) describe what it is that teachers need, in contrast to what the school may see as their needs '[Teachers] need to tap into each one's truest, unique self; to reach so that he or she has a chance to succeed; to become what every person desires to become – an effective, recognized, rewarded individual in the work setting.'

Active encouragement of all staff to express their professional individuality was imparted by leaders in the schools. *'We believe in what we're doing'*, were the strong words of the technology coordinator at Cassinia Secondary College. The staff development officer at Clematis Secondary reports, *'Wherever we can, we try and run the school in a way that makes the best use of the talent in the school.'* Kotter (1990:6) refers to developing a human network for achieving goals by 'aligning people – communicating the direction by words and deeds to all those whose cooperation may be needed so as to influence the creation of teams and coalitions that understand the vision and the strategies and accept their validity.' A replacement teacher at Boronia West High School, in his first year of practice, commented on the cooperation between his colleagues, '*Teachers get together and see how kids are going; there's always communication between teachers – always nutting it out and talking about it.*' Kotter and Bolman and Deal's words reflect the facilitating role of leaders in the participating schools who acted on a deep-seated belief in the intrinsic value of each member of staff. This belief facilitated effectiveness in their organizations. The attitudes and actions of leaders in an organization have a direct correlation to school effectiveness, as Fullan (1988:45) points out, 'Organizations do not get healthy by themselves, and we all would be extremely lucky if our organization got healthy through someone else's efforts other than our own. Managing in a non-rational world means counting on ourselves.'

Like Fullan, Rosenholtz (1989:44) also concludes that 'norms of collaboration don't simply just happen. They do not spring spontaneously out of teachers' mutual respect and concern for each other'. Fullan and Rosenholtz's conviction is confirmed in the findings of this book. What leaders in schools actually do – their behaviour, their actions, their priorities in the daily choices of administrative practice – are all critical to the development of a collaborative culture. One of the guiding attitudes of leaders in the schools in this book was the strict focus on learning and teaching as the primary and overriding role of the school. '*I think it's important to question everything you're doing if it doesn't seem to be working for every child*', the coordinator at Boronia West High School commented. A leadership focus on the centrality of teaching and learning seems critical to bringing about a stimulating professional atmosphere and increased teacher skills.

Teaching and learning is central to the culture of a fully functioning collaborative school culture. Little (1982:259) refers to a 'technical culture'. Her research demonstrated that in exceptionally effective schools:

- Teachers engage in frequent, continuous and increasingly concrete and precise talk about teaching practices;
- Teachers are frequently observed and provided with useful critiques (if potentially frightening) of their teaching;
- Teachers plan, design, research, evaluate and prepare teaching materials together;
- Teachers teach each other the practice of teaching.

Little's technical culture characterizes the cultures in most of the urban schools discussed in this book. Teaching in a mixed ability classroom, contextual learning, cooperative group work, curriculum development in a vertical structure, gender issues and student welfare are examples of the range of issues addressed. Teachers planned and evaluated their units of work jointly, worked together in teams, swapped their ideas, brainstormed difficulties and jointly problem-solved possible solutions, enabling action to be quickly taken.

A secondary teacher at Clematis Secondary enthused over jointly planned curriculum units, '*It was wonderful to work with enthusiastic people . . . we really just loved it; we liked the issues we were doing . . . you'd come out of class and think that was a really good lesson!*'

Confronting philosophical issues was also part of teacher talk. For example, at Boronia West High School a recent concern about teaching in a mixed ability classroom was raised, a philosophical curriculum stance to which the school is strongly committed. The questions raised below highlighted the central focus of teaching and learning, particularly with regard to the needs of students:

> *How are we really coping with the mixed ability classroom? Are we teaching children who come in to us, almost illiterate and innumerate, to read and count, or are we not? What about student x – it doesn't seem to be happening there. Why isn't it? What else should we be doing?* (coordinator, Boronia West High School).

The questions raised above highlighted the central focus of teaching and learning, particularly with regard to the needs of students. Solutions were sought jointly and changes worked through by the whole staff. Follow-up takes place at the fortnightly meetings. Not only did students benefit as a result, so too did teachers as their professional repertoire grew through the exchange of ideas and proposed solutions, and cooperative learning took place. At Boronia West High School collaborative leadership generated a culture of collaboration which has been perceptively described by Leithwood and Jantzi (1990:250):

> This culture is student-centred and based on norms of interaction with students that are supportive and positive; while discipline is maintained, it is obviously there to serve the interests of learning rather than an end in its own right. Teachers have a shared technical culture built on norms of collegiality, collaborative planning and continuous improvement. Staff and the student body are cohesive and have a strong sense of community. There is reciprocity between, and among, staff and students. Administrators are expected to offer instructional leadership and parents are considered co- partners in the education of students wherever possible.

However, as Little (1990) has emphasized, collaboration *per se* does not automatically serve the educational good. It can be counterproductive, for instance, by standing in the way of change and maintaining the *status quo*; it can put down students; it can serve self-interest. Therefore 'collegiality must be linked to norms of continuous improvement and experimentation in which teachers are constantly seeking and assessing potentially better practices inside and outside their own schools and contributing to other [people's practice through dissemination]' (Fullan, Bennett and Rolheiser-Bennett, 1990:223).

A strong connection between the structural frame is evident here where meeting structures and planning times set up by leaders in the school brought formal as well as informal opportunities for cooperative involvement and continuous learning for staff, which in turn led to development of educational opportunities for students.

In addition, collaborative leaders did a great deal of informal reinforcing talk to sustain and develop a collaborative culture, including praising and celebrating teachers' successes. Principals openly recognized and publicly celebrated the achievements of their staff – their innovations, their professionalism, their commitment and effort – and they encouraged them to value this in each other. '*We share our successes*', commented the integration teacher at Banksia Primary, strongly promoting the worthwhile activities of her staff. '*A pat on the back does so much more good than anything else*', comments a Year 3/4 teacher at Kennedia Primary adding that, '*well-meant praise will improve the dynamics positively*'. As Fullan and Hargreaves (1991b:48) state 'collaborative cultures are to be found everywhere in the life of the school . . . in overt praise, recognition and gratitude.' Leaders were regularly out and about in the school, particularly in the staffroom, available, talking and establishing an atmosphere where staff felt comfortable to discuss their uncertainties and seek shared solutions in an atmosphere of openness and professional honesty, illustrated here by a comment of the integration teacher at Banksia Primary:

> *Everyone shares the problem; we engender an expectation of shared responsibility. This has helped teachers and kids survive some torrid times . . . everything depends on the openness of staff; it depends on people sharing ideas and the willingness to share. They must feel what they have to share is valuable.*

These words capture Cooper's (1989:51) sentiment. 'In professional settings, when teachers are moved to share, it is usually because they are proud of something they have done with children. No amount of posturing about new roles and responsibilities can even begin to approach the powerful motivation to a professional.' In developing a collaborative culture, leaders provided strong modelling of professional cooperation and sharing by leaders in the school. A faculty head at Cassinia Secondary College describes her approach:

> *I try to be really supportive of staff. I encourage people – can I help? Is there anything I can do? Valuing other people's point of view is important too – to get people to feel wanted and be part of things – actively bringing people into the conversation.*

In keeping with Ministry of Education (1985) guidelines, establishing a formal expectation that staff will help each other is another feature of collaborative leadership. '*It's really good to come to school and know you've got support, and they'll know what you're on about*', an experienced teacher commented. Cooperation, sharing ideas, listening to and respecting others, and working in teams are part of an explicit assumption articulated by those in leadership positions. A Year 3/4 primary teacher at Kennedia Primary explains:

> *There is a school expectation here that we'll all help each other, but it's up to the individual teacher as to how we apply that expectation – it might be in the form of a unit plan or sharing extra materials – but the expectation is that we support and help each other.*

In addition to formal expectations of support, collaborative leaders recognize and give approval to informal networks of support. Support for colleagues is substantial in the collaborative school. The student welfare officer at Clematis Secondary explains:

> *Most of the staff know what each other's up to. We get on well. We enjoy each other's company. We talk a lot. We share a lot more – look for help; take advice. This leads to cooperation between staff – who teaches what, and how the school operates.*

In the present unsettling and unpredictable times of relentless educational change at both the school and system level, a collective confidence is often necessary to deal with the pedagogical and organizational complexities facing teachers. Fullan and Hargreaves (1991b:49) clarify this point: 'In collaborative cultures, teachers develop the collective confidence to respond to change quickly, selecting and adapting those elements that will aid improvement in their own work context, and rejecting those that will not.' Informal networks and a spirit of collegiality assist staff in coping effectively and cultivate a sense of camaraderie leading to a positive mood in the school and high teacher morale. Importantly, also, a cohesive staff group is engendered. According to Nias, *et al.*, (1989:74) 'help, support, trust and openness are at the heart of these [collaborative] relationships. Beneath that there is a commitment to valuing people as individuals and valuing groups to which people belong.' Collaborative leaders in this study did just this.

Leaders initiated deliberate administrative assistance for staff. Joint planning times were timetabled; visits to other classrooms within their own and others' schools were arranged opportunities; to work together outside their own classroom (e.g. camps/excursions/fetes) were organized; staff social events were regular features. School leaders took responsibility for administrative priorities in the use of space, e.g. one community staffroom/faculty classrooms located adjacent to one another. The significance of such arrangements was not lost on principals. The Principal at Clematis Secondary describes the school's staffroom as '*a central staffroom – all is one.*' The Student Welfare Officer adds, '*it's a social and a working staffroom – breeding cross fertilisation of ideas and reinforcing that view of why we're here.*'

Teachers who share a similar educational philosophy appear to have a the potential for a powerful working relationship. '*Yes! Yes! I really agree with what you're saying*', was how one young primary teacher at Kennedia

Primary School felt about a colleague's shared ideological outlook. Putting aside personality differences to focus on the task at hand, with the understanding that the interests of the students override the idiosyncrasies of individual teachers can really make a difference to school success. '*We understand why we're here; we understand there are differences amongst us all, but we manage to put that aside and work together.*'

Collaborative leaders in the project schools instituted staff norms of continuous learning. Professional development was held in high regard by school leaders. Teachers' initiatives in curriculum improvement were valued and encouraged. As a result, teachers were motivated by their view of themselves as continuing learners in their desire to promote educational success for their students. The careers teacher at Clematis Secondary shows sensitivity to the context for continuing learning. '*It takes a lot of confidence to stand up in front of your peers – standing up as the so-called expert; it's very hard to work out the balance between being the expert and being the friend, and being somebody with just another skill.*'

A teacher leader at Banksia Primary reiterated her advice to staff, '*No-one is an expert, don't give up. There's no instant solution.*' Clearly leaders' attitudes to their staff are critical if continuous learning is to become the norm, as one experienced coordinator puts it. '*The only way you can get teachers to alter their practice in their rooms is by nurturing people, giving them the professional development, and then the confidence to try it and see if it works.*' This conviction supports Barth's (1990:62) view that 'teachers can become learners and can be extraordinarily effective in stimulating and promoting the development of other teachers.' Fullan (1988:44) describes the central task of the empowered manager as that of a 'perpetual learner – when it comes to learning, effective leaders are greedy.' Cooperative inquiry is motivated by teachers' views of themselves as continuing learners, their confidence to take risks and attempt new practices. Collaborative leadership sets the context for this to take place.

Closely linked to continuing learning is a leadership milieu which empowers staff to take initiative and responsibility. Participatory decision-making, described in the structural frame in Chapter 4, ensures that those responsible for implementing a decision are included in the consultation process. The human side of this takes account of the fact that each person affected by a decision is encouraged to talk out his or her feelings and make ideas known. Strong connections exist here between the democratic organization of the structural frame and negotiation in the political frame. As a result the alienation that imposition and lack of consultation brings does not occur. Instead, a respect for diversity of opinion leads to a staff who trust each other, bonding people together in a spirit of collegiality. Professional collegiality spills over into social domains and strong friendships amongst some staff can develop. Leaders other than the principal can play a vital role in establishing the conditions for continuing learning and staff development, as one young primary teacher at Kennedia Primary School observed:

There are certain people who have fortes and influence the school other than the principal. Their personalities, their philosophical beliefs may be very, very strong in a certain area. Someone in charge of a school can ascertain where the qualities lie and, if he or she is smart, is able to draw them out. There is a real skill in seeing where the different strengths might lie, in bringing the people together, to delegate, to still be able to pull the strings in and collect the ideas, but be able to send them off to others, because then the effect runs down and it's a way of communicating that's much easier than one person sitting in the chair and playing God. Sensible leaders do that. Their strength is in being able to coordinate that.

Leaders at Kennedia Primary School modelled positive behaviours, and, as one primary teacher suggests:

There are certain people, other than the principal, who make wonderful models in certain aspects – those with fortes in curriculum development or professional development – and they influence the school; their personalities, their philosophical beliefs are very, very strong in a certain area.

Demonstrating such constructive guidance by example contributes significantly to the sustenance of a collaborative culture and to the enhancement of professional development. As Barth (1990:19) observes:

My experience suggests that as it goes between teacher and principal so shall it go in other relationships. If the teacher–principal relationship can be characterized as helpful, supportive and trusting, revealing of craft knowledge, so too will others. To the extent that teacher–principal interactions are suspicious, guarded, distant, adversarial, acrimonious, or judgmental, we are likely to see these traits pervade the school. The relationship between teacher and principal seems to have an extraordinary amplifying effect. It models what *all* relationships will be. [Barth's emphasis]

Collaborative Leadership and School Success – Human Resource Frame

Collaborative leadership, through the human resource frame, brings about a cohesive staff group, a positive mood and high teacher morale, a formal and informal network of support, a stimulating professional atmosphere, and, importantly, increased teacher skills.

Banksia Primary School specifies *cooperation and team efforts at all levels* as successful outcomes in the school. The principal there sees this as success '*in the culture of the school . . . where there is pride in work, cooperating, learning and growing as a teacher, and believing your work is important*'. This teacher culture, according to a senior teacher at Banksia Primary, has a direct impact on student learning, '*bringing about positive behaviour in kids, a feeling that school's a good place to be, and a caring response to each other*'.

Clematis Secondary's success centres around 'responding to its community and its educational needs'. It takes account of the context from which the school population is drawn and accommodates the needs of a school community with 'a trait of Mediterranean and Asian cultures for a strong emphasis on the family, with other siblings looking after younger ones.' As a result, the school has introduced a vertical structure where a mixed age range of students from Years 7 to 10 form the core class groups. Pastoral care groups are also vertically structured, incorporating family affiliations. To cater to this structure adjustments to the curriculum were necessary. The curriculum co-ordinator at Clematis Secondary explains that teacher cooperation in curriculum planning develops innovative programs specifically designed for the urban student clientele:

> *We made a conscious effort never to repeat a unit of work [because of the Year 7 to 10 structure]. We were very keen to have new things all the time – things that were current . . . every kid had new work that we prepared. Doing things like that you develop work for your clientele. You had to do things in order to stimulate/challenge – otherwise kids would be on support programs. And Year 7 to 10 in one class – you had to do things for a diverse group. In terms of accountability and looking at student outcomes, your program must reflect that. When you look at your record-keeping sheets and you see kids haven't been able to do set tasks, you have to be able to turn around and think, 'Why can't they do them?' That leads to innovation.*

At Boronia West High the human aspect operates strongly for students. A Year 9 student at Boronia West High comments, '*School works for me . . . everyone knows each other. It's like a brother and sister kind of relationship – with most of them anyway.*'

Attention to human resource aspects of leadership by leaders in the project schools led to student, teacher and organizational success through consistent monitoring of programs, innovative curriculum which caters to individual differences, and satisfied teachers who brought an enthusiastic disposition into their classroom practice. The health of these schools flourished as a result. Students were advantaged by teachers who loved their job, were professionally satisfied and stimulated, were constantly reviewing and developing their teaching practices, and who provided them with a positive atmosphere and a climate conducive to learning. Learning thrived under such conditions and the opportunity for students to realize their educational potential was maximized. Peters and Waterman (1982:240) identify this approach as being highly productive, reaping rewards for the organization, as well as the individual, 'Nothing is more enticing than the feeling of being needed, which is the magic that produces high expectations. What's more, if it's your peers that have those high expectations of you, then there's all the more incentive to perform well.'

Development of Findings

Data were gathered from interviews, extracts from school documentation, observation and the School Profile (Appendix 1). In all, forty-six subjects were interviewed from members of the school communities of the five schools studied and were drawn from an administration, teacher, parent and student base. Data was collected, reduced and reported using the Miles and Huberman (1984) interactive components of data analysis represented in Figure 4 (p. 31). The Bolman and Deal (1991) structural, human resource, political and symbolic frames provided the structure for leadership analysis. The findings of each frame are reported separately in Chapters 3, 4, 5, and 6, respectively. This chapter reports the findings of the *human resource frame*. What follows first however, are two worked through examples of the way in which primary data were transposed into the succinct findings listed below. These examples come from the human resource frame. Each finding was developed via the same process.

Example 1

Primary data

Interview response from a faculty head at Cassinia Secondary School:

> *I try to be really supportive of staff. I encourage people – can I help? Is there anything I can do? Valuing other people's point of view is important too – to get people to feel wanted and be part of things – actively bringing people into the conversation.*

Interview response from the integration officer at Banksia Primary School:

> *Everyone shares the problem; we engender an expectation of shared responsibility. This has helped teachers and kids survive some torrid times.*

Interview response from a Year 3/4 class teacher at Kennedia Primary:

> *There is a school expectation here that we'll all help each other, but it's up to the individual teacher as to how we apply that expectation – it might be in the form of a unit plan or sharing extra materials – but the expectation is that we support and help each other.*

Interview response from a secondary teacher at the Boronia West High School:

> *It's really good to come to school and know you've got support, and they'll know what you're on about.*

The primary data leads to the finding

> *Leaders in the five project schools provide an informal as well as a formal network of support.*

Example 2

Primary data

Interview response from the coordinator of Boronia West High School:

> *I think it's important to question everything you're doing if it doesn't seem to be working for every child . . . How are we really coping with the mixed ability classroom? Are we teaching children who come in to us almost illiterate and innumerate to read and count, or are we not? What about student x – it doesn't seem to be happening there. Why isn't it? What else should we be doing?*

Interview response from the student welfare officer at Clematis Secondary:

> *It's a social and a working staffroom – breeding cross-fertilization of ideas and reinforcing that view of why we're here.*

Interview response from a Year 3/4 class teacher at Kennedia Primary School:

> *Our ultimate aim is to educate the children at this school to be independent learners – to go on to high school, to go on to be social beings, to go off to the workplace. We all have to gear our minds to one thing – high school. We are all clear on our goals all this other pettiness (staff hostility you see in other schools) gets pushed aside. We need to say, 'Right, the kids are here. This is our job.'*

The primary data leads to the finding

> *Leaders who promote, develop and sustain human resource elements in their schools value teaching and learning as the primary and overriding role of the school.*

The preceding examples illustrate the kind of responses which interviewees gave to the interview questions. Responses were spontaneous and articulate, with recurring themes arising as the interviews progressed. Comments were impromptu and a congruity of responses over the nearly forty hours of interviews led to a sense of certainty and confirmation of the following generalized findings.

Findings of the Human Resource Frame

What is it that leaders do to promote, develop and sustain collaborative cultures in urban schools?

The findings of this chapter clearly indicate that collaborative leadership, which engenders a school culture fostering and promoting human resource perspectives, brings about effective teaching practice, which in turn results in great gains for students. In summary, then, leaders who promote, develop and sustain human resource elements in their schools:

- seek out the skills and talents of school community members and match these to roles and responsibilities;
- respond to the needs of individuals and accommodate these as appropriate to the overall vision of the roles and responsibilities; the school;
- value teaching and learning as the primary and overriding role of the school;
- institute staff norms of continuous learning;
- establish a formal expectation that staff will help each other;
- give approval to an informal, as well as a formal, network of support;
- provide strong modelling of professional cooperation and sharing by leaders in the school;
- encourage all staff to express their professional individuality and particular fortes in the planning of curriculum;
- establish an atmosphere of openness where staff feel comfortable to discuss their uncertainties and seek shared solutions;
- do a great deal of informal reinforcing talk.

Assist staff by:

- timetabling joint planning times;
- making visits possible to other classrooms within their own and others' schools;
- giving them opportunities to work together outside their own classroom, for example, camps/excursions/fetes;
- taking responsibility for administrative priorities in the use of space, for example, one community staffroom/faculty classrooms located adjacent to one another.

Characterized by:

- leaders who have a deep-seated belief in the intrinsic value of each individual member of staff;
- teachers who share a similar educational philosophy;
- teachers who can put aside personality differences to focus on the task at hand, with the understanding that the interests of the students override the idiosyncrasies of individual members of staff;
- a working environment of mutual support, professional acceptance and continuous learning.

How does collaborative leadership effect success in these schools?

It brings about:

- a cohesive staff group;
- a positive mood and high teacher morale;
- a formal and informal support network;
- a stimulating professional atmosphere;
- increased teacher skills;
- a sense of shared responsibility for students;
- a constantly developing curriculum.

Summary and Conclusion

It is clear that specific leadership behaviours are critical to success in developing and sustaining a collaborative culture, and to bringing about success in schools. Underpinning this leadership behaviour is the belief of school leaders that an organization's most vital resource is the talent, skill and energy of its individual members. Collaborative leaders go out of their way to celebrate and promote this. In schools, or sections of a school, where collaborative leadership is an integral part of school routine, mutual professional respect and cooperative sharing were evident, and a powerfulness was brought to the professional activity in that school which bore direct and significant results for its students. Effective leadership acknowledges the fact that schools are socially constructed; they are congregations of people where an interdependence exists between the school as an organization and its individual members. Organizations need professional experience, ideas and commitment; people need satisfying work, an income and social and personal expression. Good leadership is sensitive to this interdependence, taking active steps to meet the professional and personal needs of staff, and, at the same time, achieving school success. As Leithwood, Begley and Cousins (1992:144) conclude:

> compelling evidence suggests that collaborative school cultures contribute significantly to teacher development. Such cultures, which are 'shared' and 'technical' appear to foster practices most conducive to the types of staff (and student) development which are the focus of current school-reform efforts.

Note

1 In reference to the usage of the term 'leader' it must be noted that all interview subjects quoted in this book, whatever their title (for example, class teachers, faculty heads, integration teacher) are defined as 'leaders'.

Chapter 6

The Political Frame

Chapter 5 dealt with the human resource frame of leadership. This chapter is concerned with a further feature of collaborative leadership, namely the *political* perspective of leadership, outlined in the political frame of the Bolman and Deal (1991) typology. It is shown that leaders' understanding and management of the political milieu of school life is critical to success in the school. Far from being considered an obstacle to an effectively run school, a firm grasp of the politics of school life gives leaders a necessary tool for advancing the vision and goals it sets out to achieve.

The conceptual framework outlined several elements embraced by the political perspective:

- absence of hierarchy;
- power-sharing;
- open discussion;
- consensus;
- majority rule;
- shared responsibility;
- using authority;
- using influence;
- diffusing conflict;
- agreed-upon political behaviour;
- participatory decision-making procedures;
- disagreements not seen as disruptive;
- absence of sub-groups;
- negotiation;
- coalitions;
- networks.

This chapter will focus on these particular characteristics of collaborative leadership, though it is conceded that the other three perspectives – structure, human and symbolic – are imperative to complete the full picture. Emphasis will be given to what leaders[1] do in a political sense to achieve success in their schools.

Again, predesigned interview questions (see Appendix 2) sought out information pertinent to a particular frame of leadership, in this case, the political frame. The questions were as follows:

- In what ways is power shared in the school?
- In what preferred processes would you and other leaders engage in to ensure consensus is reached – with regard to curriculum decisions or conflict resolution? What processes would you not engage in?
- How has this fostered improvement in school outcomes – for example, in staff cohesion or student and teacher morale?
- Other?

Leadership and the Political Frame

Understandings gained from the literature inform us that the way in which leaders manage the political milieu of the school is critical to school success. Leaders use power as a means of attaining group goals and facilitating achievements. Solutions to problems can be developed through political skill and acumen, and negotiation and bargaining are all part of everyday organizational life.

If, as Bolman and Deal (1991) suggest, the goals, structure and policies of a school emerge from an on-going process of bargaining and negotiating among staff, then there is an apparent need for leaders to immerse themselves in the political milieu of the school and be sensitive to the formal and informal processes at work, if their schools are to be successful.

Acceptance of politics as inevitable in the daily life of the school acknowledges that problems will routinely arise. Leaders accept that people will have differing opinions about the way in which the issues should be resolved. Moreover, people's beliefs about the matters at hand will be fervent, and passionately held, as they are at the centre of what is closest to their hearts – their personal professional convictions. In urban schools where the state-of-play is constantly changing in terms of social welfare pressures, the demands of curriculum, a transient clientele and the structural organization of the schools themselves, matters of serious concern are continually on the agenda. Formal political processes which are seen to be fair and just provide a context in which issues can be addressed and problems solved as amicably as possible, and as part of customary practice. This doesn't mean that emotions don't run high. But it does mean that people feel they have had a fair say, and that they have had a real opportunity to be heard and have an influence. The student welfare officer at Clematis Secondary observes:

> *We operate on a structure in which significant decisions are made. Within that context people are given authority because of the fact that they are put into those positions under an elective process – it's not the fact that they've been put in by the principal or a small clique and therefore may be under suspicion.*

Decisions are readily accepted when there is a trust in the processes of an organization. Beyond the Ministry of Education 1985 guidelines, which mandated formal consultative processes, members of fully functioning collaborative schools hold an intrinsic personal belief in the sharing of power, a *commitment to power-sharing in a real way* which diffuses much of the conflict, resistance and self-protection associated with negative politics. Schools that are truly democratically organized develop positive, harmonious working relationships where the good health of the organization is protected, and as a result, allow educational issues to take centre stage. Sergiovanni (1990) quotes Kanter's (1977) view which warns of serious dangers for personal and organizational health if power is not shared and opportunities for active participation are denied to members of an organization:

> people who view their opportunity for personal growth and advancement and participation as low tend to limit their aspirations, have lower self-esteem, seek satisfaction outside work, are critical of management, are less likely to seek changes openly preferring to gripe informally and to stir the undercurrent, steer peer groups toward defensiveness and selfprotection, emphasize social relationships over tasks, be more parochial, become more complacent, and become concerned with survival and economic security rather than intrinsic aspects of the job. Persons who view themselves as low in power tend to encourage and promote low morale, be critical, behave in authoritarian ways over their own charges, seek to gain and retain control, discourage growth and opportunities of subordinates, be more insecure, and protect turf. It's pretty hard to imagine quality schooling emerging from principals, teachers, and parents who harbor these feelings and possess these characteristics. (Sergiovanni, 1990:116).

Undoubtedly there is a fusing of structural and political dimensions here which the Principal of Clematis Secondary College astutely recognizes:

> *The paradox is that there is this very democratic formal structure, but it is like a political system – everyone is playing politics along the way and trying to get something up . . . there's an open approach to everyone, a greater sense of fair play being the name of the game. No-one likes to lose on something they hold dear, but they accept it fairly well – if they don't get the vote, they don't get the vote.*

In collaboratively functioning schools, power is actively shared and decisions are reached via consensus or vote. Interestingly, of the participating schools, preference for reaching decisions by consensus or vote was divided, and not associated with a primary or secondary-based setting. Where consensus took preference, voting took place only occasionally when an agreement could not be reached. The coordinator at Boronia West High School comments:

> *Consensus can be reached via a common philosophy and a respect for what people are saying – you tend to be able to listen to someone*

> *saying something quite different from you, knowing that underlying it there are similar concerns . . . We try for consensus, we rarely have to vote. I don't like voting about matters that particularly concern people because it becomes a numbers game rather than something you've actually thought about, or can feel that your opinion is valued in any way.*

Reaching agreement through discussion, negotiation and compromise in a climate of openness, with those who might oppose or advance the educational agenda, characterizes collaboratively functioning urban schools. As a Year 9 student at Boronia West High explains, '. . . *you mostly win if it's a good point, or you get the full story . . . mostly we meet halfway and it works out.*' Power is used in a positive way to advance the vision of the school and build a stronger commitment by staff, students and parents to the implementation of decisions results. Here political realities are recognized, 'Human beings live out their daily lives and socially construct their reality through the negotiations, contractions and resistances of the rules and resources within which their lives are entwined' (Watkins, 1989:23).

In a collaborative culture, power is shared and decisions are reached via consensus or vote. Drawing on his earlier work (Watkins, 1985) and that of Giddens (1979), Peter Watkins (1989:23) asserts:

> If we are to treat people as anything other than mere ciphers or automatons blindly following a superior who has been designated or who has been taught to be a leader, then we must incorporate a view of human agency whereby people are seen to conduct their lives not as 'cultural dopes' but as knowledgeable human beings.

In terms of leadership in schools this means that people in the organization can be both dynamic participants in its operation and contributors of worthwhile professional knowledge, if they are permitted to be part of the decision-making processes. A serious obstacle to collaboration identified in this book was what was seen to be the inappropriate use of the power of veto by the principal. It is the right of school principals in Victoria to exercise the power of veto at any time at their own discretion. However, when deep-seated beliefs in power sharing and consultative processes were held by staff, the use of veto over decisions reached by vote or consensus was deeply resented. Staff felt a loss of empowerment and ownership over what was to be implemented and often withdrew their support, commitment and enthusiasm for school programs. The principal at Clematis Secondary College explains the relationship between his role and the power of veto:

> *Any ideas or actions come from the staff as a whole and the Administrative Committee administers those wishes. The principal's role is to step in and say when something is completely unacceptable. There's a veto, but normally that doesn't happen unless things are at odds with the School Council.*

And at another school, a senior teacher explains:

a few times the principal has made decisions without consultation. He hasn't appreciated that discussion is needed, but it's been OK – he just needed to know that discussion needed to be extended on controversial issues. He feels fine about that, and people feel OK about approaching him. If the principal is not approachable it creates a lot of discontent and unhappiness.

Unquestionably leaders in the project schools were overtly aware of, and cautious to avoid Watkins' (1989:27) 'critical paradigm' of educational administration which:

. . . offers the possibility of a view of educational administration which will help the school community to understand how the most 'efficient' and elaborately devised organizational planning often turns out to be a manipulative trap from which organizational members may have difficulty extricating themselves. The traditional school principal with a disproportionate degree of power was often able to create and implement such manipulative traps through the ability to shape much of the language, direct much of the discourse and guide much of the practice within the educational community.

In schools where a collaborative culture had been entrenched for some time, the principal gave credence to the obligatory need to treat the power of veto with the utmost sensitivity. However, in schools like Banksia Primary which, according to the principal, are working towards a collaborative culture, that strategy was not so straightforward. At times it was not clear-cut who should make an overriding decision – the staff through consensus, or the principal with a new vision. This scenario points to a significant tension between the principal and accountability and consensus procedures. In a school which is in the process of changing from hierarchical to collaborative decision-making sometimes consensus is not appropriate and '*things may need dictating, say, to bring curriculum into line with Ministerial guidelines*', as one young teacher at Banksia Primary maintained. Other staff seem to appreciate this dilemma. '*The buck stops with him.*' (the principal), meaning the principal must bear the responsibility of the decisions made by the staff. '*[The principal] makes the ultimate decision. It is one of his stipulated roles. Ultimately a decision has to be made by an administrator who has an overall view – not just one perspective. He carries that decision.*'
Despite these differences all of the project schools were cognizant of Watkins (1989:27) 'critical' view of politics of power and control:

By adopting a critical view of leadership within the schools, by recognizing that all human agents have some degree of knowledge, by unmasking manipulative, deceptive tactics, school administration would be founded on a more equal power basis. As a consequence many administrative practices would become demystified as the school community gained a critical understanding of those processes central to the reshaping of school administration on a more participatory, collaborative basis.

At Cassinia Secondary College voting was the strategy used to reach decisions. If voting was close, or the matter of vital concern, issues would be re-agended to allow further debate, up to three or four times if necessary. Staff meetings became *the mechanism to air views and for informal debate.* The former amalgamation in 1988 of the Technical and High Schools into the Cassinia Secondary College had left scars that were still healing at the time this research was being undertaken. It was a bitter merger, which at the time split the staff into two camps – the tech teachers on the one hand, and the high school teachers on the other. Leave as it that rift had largely healed, a degree of distrust and disaffection still remained amongst teachers. So, in terms of reaching decisions, where no ground was given by either side, a vote had to be taken. The political climate is changing as one staff member commented, '*Now people are feeling more secure and trusting of each other, we are moving towards consensus.*'

In the participating schools, leaders use power as a means of attaining group goals and facilitating achievements. Solutions to problems can be developed through political skill and acumen. Further, establishment of democratic strategies with a fair representation of views, brings about a sense of trust which, in turn, leads to an acceptance of decisions, and institutionalization of the school's purposes into the day-to-day practice. The principal of Banksia Primary School explains how it works for them . . . '*We sit down and negotiate the process to make the decision; everything is owned all the way through; understood all the way through; everyone has the opportunity to put in.*'

Negotiation and bargaining through talk and interaction are all part of everyday organizational life. Tapping into the informal network and accepting informal politics as routine assists leaders to accurately read the political mood in their school. Much informal lobbying takes place around the school and *at the pub on Friday nights.* The power of the informal network cannot be underestimated. Unchecked, it can block the formal decision-making process as one Cassinia Secondary College teacher recounts of past experience:

It's personality and skill that brings influence; it's amazing, very strong. Through conversation, chat, it's decided who gets nominated and gets support. There's lobbying power over enough staff to dictate the power groups . . . if that group don't support a decision it doesn't get through usually.

The primary data revealed that the realities of political influences are informal as well as formal with *all sorts of networks of people talking about all sorts of topics, all the time.* Constructive intervention by leaders can be made to guide energies so that they better serve the educational offerings of students. In successful schools this is achieved through people talking to one another face-to-face, informally, and formally by presenting their views openly in staff meetings. The deputy principal at Clematis Secondary makes the observation that the political process relies on people talking to each other.

> *In the open, public forum you can't manoeuvre the system, for ex-*
> *ample by presenting different faces and trying to manoeuvre the result.*
> *But here you've got to tell people frankly what you think, because in*
> *the end you've got to defend it in the public forum. You can't afford*
> *not to be honest . . . honesty is the best policy and it's just structured*
> *that way.*

Undoubtedly, strong connections exist here with the structural frame and with significant implications. *It doesn't stop people having their own cliques or interest groups, but it does stop people ruling through those,* reveals the Staff Development Officer at Clematis Secondary.

These are penetrating comments as they lie at the heart of how leaders can design a formal structure to control the informal politics of an organization, providing a constructive means of bringing important issues onto the formal agenda, and having a positive influence (for example, improved representation of women in leadership roles/innovation of curriculum). As mentioned above, it is possible for a single person or group to dominate decision-making of a school through strength of personality and/or informal power. Openness and honesty through the public forum of whole staff meetings avoids the shared values and beliefs of the school community being subverted by the negative informal lobbying of a few.

This confirms Deal and Peterson's (1990:5) belief that 'good school functioning depends on the forming of working coalitions around school purposes' and practices. However, people's affiliations can alter according to the issues at hand. '*On some issues some people are on one side, but people are changing sides all the time and are on different sides of the issues*' (deputy principal, Clematis Secondary). As one senior teacher points out, '*There are also views that people all have the same view or support the same power base. This is not the case. They may have cups of tea together, but vote quite differently.*' Professional alliances were present in all the participating schools; interest groups formed to discuss, plan and develop curriculum and organizational initiatives; networks of support were built within the school base, and staff lobbied to gain support for their projects. This involved leaders in the schools in a good deal of talking and interaction with others, '*in a lot of time talking between meetings*' (curriculum coordinator, Cassinia Secondary), and as the president of the Banksia School Council put it, '*a lot of background work physically running around*'. In addition, leaders extended their networks into the community and strong links with outside agencies and cluster school groups were maintained. There was Ministry of Education support, shared use of multicultural aides, teacher union involvement and Inner Melbourne Support Centre liaison; social welfare and police assistance was called upon as necessary. All of the schools worked actively with cluster schools, networking with their staffs, working collaboratively to enhance the resources available to all students. The pilot project Students at Risk set up in 1988 by the Cassinia/Yarra Schools Group, provides an example of such cooperation. An attitude of goodwill pervaded amongst urban schools, despite the current competitive climate for student enrolments.

A further important priority of leaders was to ensure that all information was readily available to all parties. At Banksia Primary, documentation such as school policies, or drafts of work in progress, were publicly displayed in the reception area, so that decisions being made were open for comment and input by anyone in the school community. Similarly it was seen as important at Clematis Secondary that all information was available to everyone. '*At every meeting that takes place minutes are taken and stored publicly, everybody's timetables were displayed on the board for all to see. There are no sweetheart deals. No-one gets any favours or expects them. There are no special deals on the basis of friendship or seniority.*' (senior administrator, responsible for time-tabling, rosters etc, and known as 'the daily organiser', Clematis Secondary).

The primary data demonstrates that power can only be decentralized if the individuals to whom power is entrusted have access to the information necessary to make good decisions. In the private sector, as well as in public education, much information historically has been available only at the top of the organization. If people want to make changes, they must have information of the current situation. '*Access to information is access to power*', as one member of staff at Clematis Secondary College points out. As Robbins (1989:342) states, 'When an individual in a group controls unique information, and when that information is needed to make a decision, that individual has knowledge-based power.' Opening up structures and promoting an atmosphere of open, honest communication so that knowledge is disseminated to all enabled a depth of participation in decision-making which assisted in the provision of a more equitable distribution of power. '*The main thing is to make people feel confident that even though they may not like their lot in life, it has been arrived at in a fair and equitable way*' (daily organiser, Clematis Secondary). This is significant in two ways. First, it allows for interactive, free flowing ideas thus enlarging the choices from which decisions can be made. Second, it goes a long way to eradicate the deliberate withholding of information from others in order to gain control and personal status. Eliminating the formal opportunity for such tactics strengthens a 'fairness culture' and fosters harmonious relationships in the organization. Of significance is Giddens' (1979:88) assertion that 'power is the transformative capacity through which people are capable of achieving certain outcomes.' That is, power is a relationship and not a resource. Seeing power as a relationship has far-reaching implications for leaders in the maintaining and sustaining of a collaborative school culture.

Collaborative Leadership and School Success – Political Frame

Collaborative leadership through the political frame brought about participatory decision-making procedures, power sharing, open discussions and forums, and shared responsibility for all sections of the school community. Leaders established conditions where empowerment, fair and equitable decision-making, an atmosphere of openness and a striving for consensus achieved success for their schools.

Success at Clematis Secondary College came in the form of addressing the particular educational needs of its urban clientele 'resulting in outstanding improvement in outcomes in recent years in the program as a whole'. This was accomplished through an elective system of subjects designed 'to provide students with a greater sense of empowerment over their school lives, and a greater commitment to their studies by putting the greatest degree of choice about subjects studied in the hands of students and their families'. (Response to School Profile, Appendix 1). This innovation required prudent management of change and curriculum development with political elements to the fore. Empowerment of students and parents was central to the change. The deputy principal explains how such change takes place. *'Small committees work on consensus. If they can't agree, it [the proposed change] is put up as a motion and then passed. It then goes to the staff meeting and is voted on. This process keeps the system running. It's fed by committee decisions.'* In urban schools where the pace of change was so rapid and so much was happening at once, the use of agreed-upon political behaviour by leaders facilitated open discussion, consensus or majority decisions, and diffusion of conflict, thereby enabling a commitment of staff to curriculum change and its implementation. This in turn led to enhancement of learning for students and to the success outlined above at Clematis Secondary College.

Kennedia Primary School sees part of its success lying in the organization and support of teaching and learning where:

> all members of a diverse school community work harmoniously together; where a tradition of democratic decision-making exists, where staff members are cooperative and supportive of each other; where there is on-going professional development; and where policy-writing, evaluation and review of curriculum development are established components of school organization and are working effectively. In addition, there has been innovation in the curriculum, namely a comprehensive Personal Development program, a Visual Arts program and the development of the Maths Task Centre (response to School Profile, Appendix 1).

In order to achieve this degree of success leaders at Kennedia Primary School demonstrated much political skill. Leaders ensured participatory decision-making procedures and shared responsibility were institutionalized in the school.

Authority and influence were used in constructive ways to advance the vision of the school. There was an absence of sub-groups. Creation of coalitions based on issues rather than on personalities brought a positive political influence and led to a harmonious learning environment for both students and staff. Disagreements over educational issues were seen as routine, open discussion and a valuing of others' opinions being employed by leaders to negotiate consensus decisions. Success was achieved by leaders through the active use of these political strategies. A Year 3/4 class teacher explains, '*We discuss it [the issue]. Reagenda it if necessary. Talk through the whole thing. Everyone has their say (you can't just say 'you're right, you're wrong'). People feed off that and agree or disagree.* This political climate generates positive relationships leading to cooperation and support of the introduction of new programs like those listed above, and, as result the children at Kennedia Primary school are advantaged as a result.

Politically the scene at Cassinia Secondary College was a volatile one. The way in which decisions were made, the degree to which power and responsibility was shared, the acknowledgment of the need for openness and frankness amongst staff, and the striving for consensus all had direct consequences for the development, or absence, of a collaborative culture in the school.

The political milieu at Cassinia Secondary College was vigorous as a result of the 1988 amalgamation of the Technical and High schools on the present site. Sensitive handling of decision-making was required and leaders were conscious of the need for consultation at all levels. '*The staff meeting is a mechanism to air views, and gives the opportunity to see it* [the issue] *in a different light. We give it second, third or fourth opportunities, which is much more productive than a single vote where say there's 15 for, 9 against, and the rest abstain. This* [latter situation] *is typical of low staff morale.*'

Banksia Primary School considers its success to be centred around the introduction of new approaches to the organization and support of learning and teaching. It cites 'great policies, cooperation, team efforts at all levels, open decision-making, promotion of people who are doing well, and involvement in the local community' as inclusive of its accomplishments. Leaders at Banksia Primary also focused on political elements in developing a collaborative culture in the school and achieving school success. As related in the narrative of the structural frame, decision-making was inclusive with power shared across all sectors of the school community. Promotion of democratic processes led to wide representation and leadership responsibility. It also allowed people to express their opinions and to feel that they were given a fair hearing. Leaders provided an open, supportive environment encouraging the sharing and challenging of ideas. Having had the opportunity to influence the outcome of a decision, staff, students and parents were more accepting of it and gave greater commitment to its implementation. Skills of negotiation and appropriate exercising of authority by leaders assisted the process. Changes in policy were thus institutionalized bringing success to the school. As well, success in establishing cooperation and team efforts eventuated.

Development of Findings

Findings of the political frame were established using the same methodology as that of the other three frames. Miles and Huberman's (1984) inter-active model provided the means by which the large volume of primary data, collected from interviews, documentation, observation and the School Profile (Appendix 1) was categorized and analysed. These data were revisited many times, being classified and reclassified until eventually the findings were refined to the distilled form presented below. Figure 4 (p. 31) shows the approach. Data was organized into the structural, human resource, political and symbolic elements of the Bolman and Deal (1991) typology. Findings from *each frame* were then generalized. The findings of the *political frame* are presented in this chapter. What follows first, however, are two worked-through examples of the way in which primary data were transposed into the succinct findings listed below. These examples come from the political frame. Each finding was developed via the same process.

Example 1

Primary data

Interview response from the daily organiser at Clematis Secondary College:

> *Information is the most important thing and information at this school is available to everybody. At every meeting that takes place minutes are taken and stored publicly. Everybody's timetable, everyone's allotment, is displayed on the noticeboards for everyone to read. There are no sweetheart deals, nobody can say this person's getting favours that we don't know about, because it's all public. Nobody gets any favours or expects them. It's extremely important that people don't feel there are any special deals for people on the basis of friendship or seniority; and it's also important so that people understand the methods that are used to administer the place. If people want to make changes that sort of information is essential because you can't propose a change unless you know how the current system is operating.*

Interview response from the principal of the Banksia Primary School:

> *Proposals for curriculum policy have to go to staff, and have to go to the school community. To go to the school community what we actually do is run off about 20 copies of the proposal and put them on the front bench. Then we just put in the newsletter (we have a newsletter that goes home to everyone) that 'there are copies of a proposed language policy and possible program on the front bench, and if you're interested would you take one and read it' – and people do, and they comment on it.*

Interview response from the Year 5/6 class teacher at Kennedia Primary School:

> *The newsletter is pretty informative. We print important things in other languages. We have a set time when the multicultural teacher aides are all here and are available to speak with parents on the phone or face-to-face. Parents read something in the newsletter (and it's got to be written in other languages) and it says 'if you want know more about this, ring on Tuesday afternoon.'*

The primary data leads to the finding

> *Politically astute collaborative leaders in inner city schools ensure all information is accessible to all.*

Example 2

Primary data

Interview response from the principal of the Banksia Primary School:

> *We sit down and negotiate the process to make the decision; everything is owned all the way through; understood all the way through; everyone has the opportunity to put in.*

Interview response from the principal of the Clematis Secondary College:

> *Anyone can put up a motion about anything they like, anytime they like.*

Interview response from the president of the School Council of the Banksia Primary School:

> *As a parent I see the organization in the sense that it is an open school, that we are welcome at any time . . . you don't feel that if there is a problem you can't go in . . . so there's an openness, there's a sense of belonging that's built up that this is our school, this is our community.*

Interview response from a Year 3/4 class teacher at Kennedia Primary School:

> *Band 3/4 teachers have the power. But newer teachers are encouraged . . . the seniors promote your right to have your view.*

The primary data leads to the finding

> *Leaders in the project school foster active participation by all sectors of the school community in the decision-making process.*

The above examples are illustrative of the replies of leaders in the schools to the interview questions. There was a recurring pattern in the responses and a consistency over the nearly forty hours of interviews which led to a certitude and authenticity of the following generalized findings.

Findings of the Political Frame

What is it that leaders do to promote, develop and sustain collaborative cultures in urban schools?

The above discussion leads to some generalizations about what it is that leaders do, via political processes, to promote, develop and sustain collaborative cultures in urban schools. Politically astute, collaborative leaders:

- see political processes as part of everyday school life;
- foster active participation by all sections of the school community in the decision-making processes;
- promote open forums, where points of view are defended publicly, avoiding negative manipulation of the decision-making process;
- reach agreement through consensus wherever possible;
- vote on decisions that cannot be reached by consensus;
- exert positive influence in an informal way by lobbying or outcomes which will advance the educational agenda;
- ensure all information is accessible to all.

Characterized by:

- an openness and honesty in presenting points of view;
- showing respect for, and attention to, people's points of view;
- a sharing of power;
- a preparedness to accept decisions made by majority rule;
- a satisfaction that the system is fair.

How does collaborative leadership effect success in these schools?

It brings about:

- well thought through decisions;
- a stronger commitment by staff, student and parents to the implementation of decisions;
- a sense of trust;
- an advancing of the educational agenda.

Summary and Conclusion

Far from being negative or destructive in the organization, political elements of collaborative leadership in this book emerge as contributing to sound organizational health and an advancing of the educational agenda. Leaders in the participating schools took active steps to ensure an absence of hierarchy, empowerment of teachers, students and parents, open and frank discussion and a striving for consensus. Political skills of lobbying, negotiation, positive use of authority and the diffusion of conflict, led to a positive influence and successful student, teacher and organizational outcomes. Political processes were seen as part of everyday school life and leaders fostered an active participation by members of the school community in the decision-making process. As a result, decisions were well thought through, a sense of trust was engendered, and commitment of staff, students and parents to the implementation of decisions was strong.

Note

1   In reference to the usage of the term 'leader' it must be noted that all interview subjects quoted in this book, whatever their title (for example, class teachers, faculty heads, integration teacher) are defined as 'leaders'.

Chapter 7

The Symbolic Frame

Chapter 6 presented insights into the political frame of leadership in a collaborative culture. Chapter 7 addresses the fourth frame of the Bolman and Deal (1991) thesis, namely the symbolic frame. Each of the four frames – structural, human resource, political and symbolic – brings particular and peculiar understandings to the study of leadership in an organization. The specific contribution of the symbolic frame is the attention it gives to the *shared* understandings that run beneath the surface of organizational life, often submerged and overlooked. In a sense they are out of sight and this makes them particularly elusive and hard to capture, or indeed, even articulate. Leaders who can read between the lines of the symbolic frame are in an enviable position. For, from that enlightened position they can nurture and promote the beliefs and values embedded in school life, and take action to portray them through symbols, rituals and ceremonies. Schools are full of symbolic happenings and events. Leaders who can recognize their significance then have the potential to exploit their capacity to bring success to their school.

The conceptual framework outlined in Chapter 2 identified several distinctive elements of the symbolic frame:

- beliefs;
- values;
- attitudes;
- norms of behaviour;
- shared meanings;
- symbols;
- rituals;
- ceremonies.

This chapter discusses the symbolic aspects of collaborative leadership, making an explicit distinction between symbolic perspectives and the broader culture in which they reside. Mention is made of the unique demands facing urban schools in Melbourne at the present time, and of the personal as well as organizational values and beliefs that prevail in successful schools. Findings have been synthesized from this analysis providing specific student, teacher and organizational outcomes.

Although the very nature of the symbolic aspects of the culture of a school makes it difficult to isolate, Nias, *et al.* (1989:11) see it as important to disentangle their identifiable features and propose the following as essential characteristics of the symbolic frame – beliefs, values, understandings, attitudes, meanings and norms (arrived at by interaction); and symbols, rituals and ceremonies. Conceptually delineating the symbolic frame in this way is useful in drawing out the specific features of what is otherwise a non-specific area of study.

In terms of conceptualizing the symbolic perspective, it is important to distinguish it from the notion of *culture*. In many writings associated with leadership theory, culture is seen as synonymous with values, beliefs, shared meanings, symbols, rituals and ceremonies. While acknowledging that the two are closely aligned, the position taken here is that symbolic aspects do not *equal* culture. In this book, collaborative culture is interpreted in a broader context which importantly *includes* the symbolic frame, but also embraces structural, human resource and political perspectives. It mirrors Richard Bates' (1993:3) revealing interpretation which links symbolic aspects to action:

> Culture is what gives meaning to life. Culture is the intellectual framework that connects beliefs, values and knowledge with action. Culture is sedimented deeply into the unconciousness of individuals through routinisation of action. Administration is part of the process and facilitates or inhibits collective action through the mobilisation of resources and the routinisation of action. Administration inevitably, therefore, not only produces and reproduces, but it is also saturated with cultural concerns.

This specifics of my delineation of cultural elements have been set out in the conceptual framework outlined in Chapter 2, which details further discussion as to what it is that encompasses a collaborative culture. But for now, one feature, namely, the *symbolic perspective*, is addressed.

The symbolic aspects of an organization comprise beliefs and values, attitudes and norms of behaviour. These are embedded in the day-to-day activities of a school and are represented in symbols, rituals and ceremonies. The questions asked of the staff, parent and student leaders[1] in the five project schools with regard to the symbolic frame were:

- What *shared* values run through the daily activities of school life?
- What do you and other leaders do to preserve and promote those values – say, in the traditions and symbols of the school, or, informally?
- How has this brought about the successes achieved in the school?
- Other?

The questions for the symbolic frame proved to be difficult to answer as, by definition, the symbolic elements are elusive and difficult to articulate. Leaders in schools know they must work simultaneously on staff needs and skills, on goals and roles and the dynamics of political power and conflict. But there is something else that operates beyond all of these, an intangible manifestation that reflects the ethos of the school. It embodies the shared values that run through the school. It is a strong undercurrent which flows beneath the surface, giving meaning to and shaping the daily choices and priorities of school activities. It brings a propelling power to the decisions being made in the school, and yet it is largely unarticulated. It is not surprising, therefore, given the implicit, tacit nature of shared meanings and norms operating in a school setting, that subjects found the answers to the above questions far from straightforward. As a senior teacher at Banksia Primary replied, *'I can't really put my finger on it – it's a sort of feeling.'* Likewise from the deputy principal at Cassinia Secondary College, *'I suppose there is a bottom line but I haven't identified it yet!'* As a result of such responses, the questions of the symbolic frame were modified and generalized. The results, therefore, have been derived from a wider variety of discussion arising from extended questions about values and beliefs, often ranging across the other frames of reference – human, political and structural.

Leadership and the Symbolic Frame

Results indicate that there is a deeply ingrained, common thread of shared belief which guides the practice of those working successfully in urban schools of Melbourne. It is central to the work done in these schools and embodies an unswerving commitment to the children in their care. It goes beyond the academic domain of teaching and learning into the social context of students. It is the expression of these values by leaders in the school which brings the symbolism alive. Leaders promote and protect these beliefs through the leadership behaviour of the structural, human resource and political frames, outlined in the foregoing chapters, which institutionalizes the vision of the school, grounding the underpinning beliefs in the school's daily routines and activities.

The research discloses that leaders in the project schools held certain beliefs, values and attitudes. Unlike the other three frames, findings indicated that, in the symbolic frame, it was not so much what leaders did that was significant but what they believed in. Not so much what strategies were used but what norms of behaviour were instituted, and what symbols, rituals and ceremonies represented them. Hence the leadership behaviour in this frame is not reported as what leaders *did* to achieve success in their schools, but what beliefs and values were *held*, what attitudes and norms of behaviour were instituted as a result, and what symbols, rituals and ceremonies depicted them.

School leaders in this investigation have a deeply held belief that disadvantaged children should have full educational opportunities and that school arrangements can make this happen.

There's something about working in an inner city suburban area dominated by ethnic groups – you can't help but have an admiration for the way they get on with living. They have a wonderful sense of supporting each other. The staff see that, and think 'these kids deserve every chance' and feel 'it's my responsibility to give them my best' (student welfare coordinator, Clematis Secondary).

The deputy principal at Clematis Secondary saw the leadership of his school as:

Trying to do the best job you can taking into account that we're working with migrant working-class students . . . there's a strong feeling that these kids are getting a rough deal in the society and we want to do what we can to help them as much as possible . . . whoever they are we'll take them in and give them a go, and the best we can give them is a good education.

There is a strong conviction that schooling can educate these students in ways that will provide them with greater choice in their future lives, particularly in terms of their tertiary education or job opportunities. Supported and encouraged by the principal and other leaders, teachers aim to cater to the individual needs of their students, be they social, emotional or academic; to organize their curriculum and school structures accordingly, and to provide the best possible start for students in their adult life. They are vigilant and united in their efforts to realize these goals.

We are all striving to equip the kids as best we can, so when they go on to post-primary, when it comes to choices, and when they come to get a job, it's a job that they have chosen, and not something they have to accept . . . Every kid gets a chance to do their best. Every child is cared for. All teachers know all the kids in the school. All children relate to all the teachers in the school. There's a pretty nice feeling operating between teachers and children (Year 5/6 teacher, Kennedia Primary School).

Similarly the coordinator at Boronia West High expresses a shared belief in the welfare of the whole school community: '*the welfare of students, of staff and of parents, plus children in this area.*'

Without exception, these types of comments dominated the responses made to the questions posed of the symbolic frame. Leaders were deeply committed to the particular needs of a student populations they served, and were prepared to meet the challenges that this brought. Leaders in the project schools were the guardians and proponents of these shared beliefs. As Nias, *et al.* (1989:73) indicate, these attitudes 'arise from and embody a set of social and moral beliefs about desirable relationships between individuals and the community of which they are a part, not from beliefs about epistemology and pedagogy.' When the student welfare coordinator at Clematis Secondary comments, '*I don't agree with all the teaching methods of the various people, but*

I would never doubt their commitment to doing the best for the kids', it is clear that social and moral values are to the fore, rather than pedagogical ones.

Apart from their deep-seated commitment to social justice issues, leaders in the project schools held a strong personal conviction to and belief in the democratic process. *'An autocratic approach will not serve these kids,'* commented the principal of Clematis Secondary College. *'Our shared belief is that we have a shared belief; we're not constrained by the bureaucracy,'* another teacher from the same school remarked. The integration teacher at Banksia Primary School speaks of *'a fair go for everybody'*. Such strongly held beliefs drive the broader context in which the educational agenda sits, providing what Starratt (1991:187) calls 'an ethical environment for the conduct of education'. Clearly there are strong overlaps here with the structural, human resource and political frames, directed by an underpinning commitment, belief and trust in the democratic process, an openness and a sense of belonging, and a respect and valuing of all members of the school community. In addition, leaders in these urban schools had an overriding belief that each individual, particularly each individual student, is of intrinsic worth. A teacher at Boronia West High makes this observation:

> *People aren't streamed. Everyone is an equal human being. There's no better or worse person than any other person. And they should be given the most opportunities from their schooling to help them determine where their own personal directions are. It's not like the old system where they're graded. They're not a percentage, they're human beings. They're catered for. The individualness comes out and is promoted.*

Associated with this is the care and commitment of leaders who put students as people first, and members of the school second. It is an acknowledgment that often social welfare needs of students are greater than educational ones. The principal of Clematis Secondary College elaborates, *'the academic regime by itself is not sufficient. The social aspect must be attended to before the academic can take place . . . you've got to be tuned to a wider agenda.'* The student welfare coordinator at Cassinia Secondary College confirms this view:

> *The amount of work that goes into looking after all the different cultures of kids is enormous . . . kids are encouraged from every background to do well. We all give them as much help as we possibly can.*

A caring, supportive attitude is interwoven with social justice attitudes. Students respond to school when leaders have their interests at heart, as a Year 9 student at Boronia West High, who has left home, demonstrates:

> *When school's over everyone rushes out. Here we stay till school closes . . . when you've got nowhere to go, if you don't have a school to go to, where do you go? It's a tremendous help when you know it's always there for you and they'll do their best for you.*

Such a school climate is not simply achieved by believing in it. Elements of the structural, human resource and political frames play a contributing role. Participatory decision-making (structural), acceptance of the individual (human resource), diffusion of conflict (political), as well as a norm of interpersonal openness of the symbolic frame are all interwoven to achieve success in schools. Again, it is worth noting the important way in which the structural, human resource and political frames are inextricably tied to each other via the underpinning beliefs and values of the symbolic frame.

Comment needs to be made at this point about the turbulent world of urban schools in Melbourne at the time of this research. In addition to the ongoing complexities inherent in the education of students of low socio-economic, transient, non-English speaking backgrounds, schools were being faced with amalgamation, school closures, staff dislocation, daily changes in school management procedures, and the dismantling of school support services. Cassinia Secondary School was closed within nine months of data gathering for this project. Needless to say, times are tough in these schools and imaginative and courageous leadership is required. So it needs to be emphasized that the *caring, sharing*, and *harmonious* aspects of a collaborative culture outlined in these findings are not ones of quaint motherhoodness where *caring and sharing* takes the form of a storybook attitude where everything in the garden is rosy, and staff and children skip off happily at the end of another perfect day! It is not a happily-ever-after scenario. On the contrary, a context of high drama is often the reality. The symbolic perspective brings real insights to bear in this discussion, because what is of significance here is that when leaders become the keepers and spokespersons of the values, attitudes and beliefs shared by the school community, the drama can be identified and better managed. Schools will always be places of intensity and drama because they are social organizations whose reason for being is grounded in values and higher societal purposes. Understanding the symbolic perspectives will never eliminate the drama, and that is not the aim; drama, like politics, is inevitable, and, when grasped and comprehended, can be used to advantage. Starratt (1993:41) proposes that 'leadership involves the playing of the drama with greater intensity, with greater risk, with greater intelligence, with greater imagination, with greater dedication to making it work.' It would seem that successful leaders in the schools had just these skills and personal attributes, something that Fullan and Hargreaves (1991b:9) refer to as 'personal courage', and Fullan (1991:29) calls 'practising fearlessness'. Drama is certainly a central part of these schools' daily milieu, and it is interesting to observe that despite this, and possibly *because* of it, caring and valuing of people, fairness and support, are all very much part of the embedded practices. As well, formal support for collegiality is given at the government level, where, amongst other characteristics, The Schools Council in its 1990 publication, *Australia's Teachers: An Agenda for the Next Decade*, states that 'good schools have the staff working collegially and sharing in decision making, and they have a say about important issues which concern their work' (Schools Council, 1990:72).

Symbols, rituals and ceremonies all held a strong place in the culture of the participating schools. Symbols of *participation* and *community* were present in the project schools. At Kennedia Primary, for example, leaders ensured that documents were written in every language, as were signs around the school, clearly showing the respect for the ethnicity of the community groups in the school. Valuing of diversity was symbolized in a painted mural on the school wall depicting the diverse multicultural nature of the school community. Food was a hallmark of the multicultural background of the Kennedia Primary school population with curriculum nights, The Annual General meeting, staff celebrations, indeed all major events, being celebrated with a shared spread of ethnic specialities prepared by the school families. Staff, too, enjoyed sharing their favourite foods around the staffroom table at lunchtimes. Food has become a symbol of the school's culture. At Banksia Primary there was a strong sense of participation and community in the school and this was symbolized by a beautiful patchwork wall hanging made by the combined efforts of the whole school community. The principal at Banksia Primary cites the symbolism of participation, *'we all own it. We can point to our bit, and we all feel good about it.'*

Interpersonal openness was a powerful feature of the Boronia West High School and leaders in that school community were masters of its practice. The school building itself is an embodiment of a close school community, but of particular interest, as a symbol of the school's egalitarian philosophy, is the large central meeting hall which forms a focal hub for interaction, and where space is shared jointly between staff and students. There is no exclusive space here for students or for staff; no staffroom, no student common room; teachers are referred to on a first-name basis. The physical arrangements of the school building symbolize the educational ideology.

Deal and Kennedy (1982:15) describe the rituals of organizations as elements in the culture as:

> systematic and programmed routines of day-to-day life in the company. In their mundane manifestations – which we call rituals – they show employees the kind of behaviour that is expected of them. In their extravaganzas – which we call ceremonies – they provide visible and potent examples of what the company stands for.

The same can be said of the rituals and ceremonies in the participating schools. On a routine basis the ritual of meeting times set up by leaders enabled staff, students and parents to share in, and be influenced by the school ethos. School Council, whole staff meetings, curriculum and faculty committees and Student Representative Council meetings were particularly important. So too was the more informal ritual time spent by staff in the staffroom at breaks, lunchtimes and after school. School assemblies were also significant rituals in Deal and Kennedy's terms as they provided vehicles for the articulation of the school's values and beliefs. Leaders in the project schools were attentive to the significance of these rituals, organizing meetings, running assemblies, chatting informally, and socializing in the times in between. Interpersonal openness was a norm. All these occasions provided opportunities for infusing the values and beliefs of the school. In addition, leaders in the schools developed and sustained a collaborative culture through special celebrations. Festivals, such as the multicultural festival held at Cassinia Secondary, and the centenary celebration at Banksia Primary brought a focused, demonstration of the values and beliefs which these schools stand for and so earnestly promote.

The symbolic dimension of the collaborative cultures in the project schools became operative via the active and overt promotion of specific beliefs, values and attitudes promoted by their leaders, and by the symbols, rituals and ceremonies which demonstrated them. As a result, norms of behaviour which embodied these beliefs, values and attitudes were institutionalized into the daily practice of the schools. Successful leaders striving to develop, maintain and sustain a collaborative culture brought rationality to this otherwise irrational frame through explicitly identified beliefs and values, the capacity to interact with others to articulate, reinforce and consummate them in public ceremonial forums, and routine events. This meant that leaders in the project schools were able to operate on two levels at once – 'on an intellectual level to develop a personal educational philosophy; and on a practical day-to-day basis, influencing others by example and action' (Bolman and Deal, 1991:253).

Collaborative Leadership and School Success – Symbolic Frame

As discussed previously in this chapter, leaders actively communicated a deep-seated belief that disadvantaged children should have full educational opportunities. In actively advancing this belief, leaders were able to gain the commitment of staff to this end with resulting successful student outcomes. In the case of Banksia Primary this was in the form of new approaches to the organization and support of learning via policies and programs, maximizing the potential for learning for students. *'We give them the best possible curriculum activities we've got. The parents are lucky that they've got a group of teachers who for 98% of the time put their children above everything else'* (Year 1/2 class teacher). Clearly there are direct connections here between the beliefs held by leaders in the school and school success. Once again the interrelationships between the frames is evident. The symbolic element of beliefs is intertwined with the human resource elements of cooperation and support with the resulting organizational outcome of staff commitment and institutionalization of vision.

These interrelationships are described by Susan Moore Johnson, (1990:217):

> Individuals who might otherwise pursue personal interests commit themselves to the organization and adopt its principles and purposes,

often giving more than ordinary effort and devising ways to reduce discord, minimize differences, and work cooperatively. They interpret their contributions and rewards in the light of the organization and its accomplishments.

Kennedia Primary cites part of its school's success as having '*a commitment to social justice issues*' (response to School Profile). Leaders there, as in the other project schools, ensure that social justice values are determining the culture of their schools, where student populations are dominated by transient, low socio-economic, migrant backgrounds with English as the second language for many students.

At Boronia West High School, the tradition of success has been to tackle 'the widening gulf between society and its educational institutions' (Middleton, 1982:60). This tradition has been maintained during its twenty-year history, as the coordinator explains, '*I've been here for ten years and the school's changed a lot in ten years, but our local community's changed a lot too. The school changes all the time. It evolves.*' Integral to Boronia West High's success has been the capacity of its leaders to respond to change and meet the individual needs of its students by providing a non-mainstream setting with egalitarian relationships between staff and students. Leadership density underpins the organization of the school. No title of 'principal' exists. An elected 'coordinator' is the formal leader of the school and decisions are made by the staff as a whole. In this sense all teachers in the school are leaders. This breadth of leadership which permeates the school results directly in innovation in the curriculum. Staff meet regularly to discuss the needs of each student and intervention in the form of new or modified approaches to programs, or changes in management or organization of the learning context, takes place. This has resulted in sustained achievement over many years. This translation of the values and beliefs held by leaders into the practices of the school has brought success. A Year 12 student at Boronia West High explains the relationship between a school environment where leaders show respect for students, and its direct link to positive student behaviour and development of learning, that is, school success:

> *The lack of respect some teachers have for students generates the immaturity of students* (speaking of her experience at another school). *When they do come to this school, they stop being 5-year-olds and start becoming people – which makes a difference. It not only makes a difference to them but makes a difference to their learning, and, it makes a difference to the class.*

It is the beliefs and values held by leaders in these schools and the vigilance with which they were translated into the school's daily activities that resulted in success for students, teachers and the organization. For example, an appreciation of diversity was a fundamental value held by leaders in the schools. The Year 5/6 teacher at Kennedia Primary describes the connections between a valuing of diversity, curriculum and success:

We've got 28 families [in the school] who are Australian. Only 28!
. . . Throughout the school there is a valuing of all those other com-
munities. I mean we who are in the minority [Australians] do value
that, and do listen to that. And that is a very strong part of the
curriculum. But there's another funny thing to it, that it's just ac-
cepted. I mean I find that the kids in particular really have got a very
good knowledge, considering their age and their experience, of differ-
ent cultures. Also they have got a very, very accepting attitude of all
those differences. And, you know, we don't have any racial problems
amongst the school or finger-pointing, or anything like that, and I
know that exists in other places . . . A lot of our curriculum hinges
around differences – I don't know what it is . . . it's just there and it
underwrites everything we do and it just becomes part of your ap-
proach to the kids, and I think people value that.

Valuing diversity and caring for each other extends into the adult domain. The caring aspect takes account of each other as professionals. '*When you tell everyone, "I need help", everyone helps you,*' explains a young primary teacher from Kennedia Primary School. '*This is a caring, happy place to come to; a place where there is respect,*' commented another member of that school's staff. School success is achieved when teachers are happy in their work, and when teacher morale is high and leads to strong staff commitment. These may be indirect outcomes, but as the staff development coordinator at Clematis Secondary points out, '*If the staff are happy, they spend less time fighting and more time on educational issues, like developing the curriculum.*'

Direct links can be seen between intrinsic valuing of each individual, student or staff member and school success at Kennedia Primary where part of that school's success is centred around 'all members of a diverse school community working harmoniously together' (response to the Kennedia Primary School Profile). The affirmation of leaders in respecting and valuing each individual member of the school community rubs off on teachers, parents and students, effecting an absence of racial tension and a harmonious school climate, a significant outcome considering the circumstances facing urban schools (in one school there are 17 different nationalities). '*Teachers take a great deal of pride in the fact that there is no conflict between the children in the school grounds, or in the classroom,*' comments the principal of Kennedia Primary School.

Clematis Secondary nominated itself for its success in addressing a particular problem, namely 'responding to its community and accommodating its educational needs', resulting in outstanding improvements in outcomes in recent years in the program of the school as a whole. This is evident in the elective system of subjects designed 'to provide students with a greater sense of empowerment over their school lives, and a greater commitment to their studies by putting the greatest degree of choice about subjects studied in the hands of students and their families' (response to School Profile). In responding to its community and accommodating its educational needs leaders at Clematis Secondary were directed by the belief that disadvantaged children should have full educational opportunities. As a result they instigated certain school arrangements, such as student choice in the curriculum which maximized their students' learning. Leaders also ensured that provision was made for social welfare support for students acknowledging their special needs, which assisted in developing a climate conducive to learning and a development of educational potential. In these ways the stated school success was achieved.

Development of Findings

Findings of the symbolic frame were drawn from the whole body of data gathered from each of the forty-six interviewees, school documentation and observation, and categorized into the four frames. What follows are two worked through examples of the way in which primary data were transposed into the succinct findings listed below. These examples come from the symbolic frame. Each finding was developed via the same process .

Example 1

Primary data

Interview response from a Year 5/6 class teacher at Kennedia Primary School:

> *Every kid gets a chance to do their best. Every child is cared for. All teachers know all the kids in the school. All children relate to all the teachers in the school. There's a pretty nice feeling operating between teachers and children.*

Interview response from a Year 9 student at Boronia West High School:

> *When school's over everyone rushes out. Here we stay till school closes . . . when you've got nowhere to go, if you don't have a school to go to, where do you go? It's a tremendous help when you know it's always there for you and they'll do their best for you.*

Interview response by the president of the School Council at Banksia Primary School:

> *We want to create an environment where kids learn to think and to care about themselves, other people and property.*

The primary data leads to the finding

> *Leaders in the project schools created an attitude of caring and respect:*

Example 2

Primary data

Interview response from the curriculum coordinator at Cassinia Secondary College:

> *The amount of work that goes into looking after all the different cultures of kids is enormous . . . kids are encouraged from every background to do well. We all give them as much help as we possibly can.*

Interview response from the deputy Principal Clematis Secondary College:

> *Trying to do the best job you can taking into account that we're working with migrant working-class students is what we are on about . . . There's a strong feeling that these kids are getting a rough deal in the society and we want to do what we can to help them as much as possible . . . whoever they are we'll take them in and give them a go, and the best we can give them is a good education.*

Interview response from the Year 1/2 class teacher at Banksia Primary School:

> *We give them the best possible curriculum activities we've got. The parents are lucky that they've got a group of teachers who for 98% of the time put their children above everything else.*

The primary data leads to the finding

> *Leaders in the project schools were guardians and proponents of a belief that disadvantaged children should have full educational opportunities and that school arrangements can make this happen.*

Findings of the Symbolic Frame

The preceding examples reflect the pattern of responses which repeatedly emerged from the interviewees. Comments were unprompted and immediate, expressed with clarity and coherence. The consistency of responses over the nearly forty hours of interviews led to a certainty and confirmation of the following generalized findings. As a result of deductive analysis of the above primary data and the understandings gained from the related theory and research the following breakdown of findings has been identified.

What is it that leaders do to promote, develop and sustain collaborative cultures in urban schools?

Leaders in the project schools were the guardians and proponents of the following identified shared beliefs and values:

Beliefs
- a belief that disadvantaged children should have full educational opportunities and that school arrangements can make this happen;
- a belief in the democratic process.

Values
- an intrinsic valuing of each individual; student or staff member;
- valuing of diversity;
- a valuing of community;
- a valuing of participation.

How does collaborative leadership effect success in these schools?

It brings about the institutionalization of the following attitudes and norms:

Attitudes
- acceptance of differences;
- caring and respect;
- egalitarianism;
- inclusiveness;
- self-worth.

Norms of:
- interaction;
- cooperative/team approach;
- mutual support;
- staff, student and parent cohesion;
- interpersonal openness;
- sharing;
- commitment/enthusiasm.

Symbols, Rituals and Ceremonies
- Leaders articulated the beliefs and values of the school through symbols, rituals and ceremonies.

Summary and Conclusion

The symbolic frame contains the beliefs, values and attitudes of leaders, denoting and directing the fundamental purposes and processes of the school. Through these beliefs, values and attitudes leaders established structures for the management and organization of the school, regarded people in certain ways and saw politics as routine. In a collaborative school culture leaders established democratic decision-making processes, treated people collegially, and sought consensus as a priority. Norms of interaction, cooperation and teamwork, mutual support, interpersonal openness and commitment resulted and the primary purposes of the school were achieved. Symbols, rituals and ceremonies bore formal representation of the school's ideology. Critical to success was the interplay of the symbolic with the structural, human resource and political frames. In the case of the five urban schools in this study, beliefs and values centred around a valuing of diversity, an acceptance of the individual, a strong sense of participation and community and a commitment by staff to fully support students from disadvantaged backgrounds, socially and academically, so that the educational potential of each child could be maximized and their life choices optimized.

Note

1   In reference to the usage of the term 'leader' it must be noted that all interview subjects, whatever their title (for example, class teacher, faculty head, teacher aide) are defined as 'leaders'.

Chapter 8

Further Connections

The Hypothesized Causal Links

A most interesting configuration started to present itself as a consequence of the analysis of the findings reported in the previous four chapters. Reflection on the findings produced powerful causal connections emerging between collaborative leadership and student, teacher and organizational outcomes. A constantly recurring pattern in the responses, and a consistency over the forty hours of interviews, supports the authenticity of these connections. Significantly, these emerging patterns aligned closely with the findings of the related theory and literature linking leadership behaviour and school success, discussed in Chapter 1. In response to this revelation, I undertook a hypothesizing process to elicit greater insight into the interconnections between what leaders *did* in their daily practice in schools and how this led to *achievement* of success, the underlying premise being that these interrelationships could form the springboard for predictable pathways to outcomes for students, teachers and the organization. This being the case, some reasonably accurate forecasting of cause and effect relationships could be made. Importantly, then, leaders in schools could track their leadership actions and behaviour, following them through to their particular consequences for students, staff and the organization. Being able to do this is a significant step in leadership practice, bringing a clear, practical, analytical way of identifying the results of individual leadership on outcomes for the school. As a result, hypothesized causal links were made and categorized as *structural, human resource, political and symbolic*, using the Bolman and Deal (1991) frames. Success was categorized as *student, teacher and organizational* outcomes.

Some examples of this process are listed below:

Example 1

Primary data

> *It [the teaching and learning approach] helps you to find out who you are as an individual . . . students take responsibility for themselves in their self-development and their learning . . . staff are there to assist, not to control.*

Elements deduced from primary data

- student opportunity for self-expression;
- student choice in the curriculum;
- staff support for students;
- positive student/teacher relations

Leads to the hypothesized structural student outcome

Leadership density $\Rightarrow$ student empowerment $\Rightarrow$ climate conducive to learning $\Rightarrow$ development of educational potential.

Example 2

Primary data

> It was wonderful to work with enthusiastic people . . . we really just loved it. We liked the issues we were doing . . . you'd come out of class and think 'that was a really good lesson.'

Elements deduced from the primary data

- respect for and cooperation with co-workers;
- high teacher morale;
- belief in curriculum program;
- professional satisfaction.

Leads to the hypothesized human resource teacher outcome

Organizational fit $\Rightarrow$ personal/professional expression $\Rightarrow$ stimulating practice $\Rightarrow$ high morale $\Rightarrow$ love of teaching.

Example 3

Primary data

> It [the formal democratic decision-making process] *doesn't stop people having their own cliques or their own interest groups, but it does stop people ruling through those.*

Elements deduced from the primary data

- formal democratic processes;
- acknowledgment of informal political network;
- monitoring of 'power-play' through formal structures.

Leads to the hypothesized political organizational outcome

Acceptance of politics as routine ⇒ problems/conflicts seen as inevitable ⇒ awareness of the informal political network ⇒ opportunity for the diffusion of conflict ⇒ good organizational health.

Example 4

Primary data

> *People aren't streamed. Everyone is an equal human being. There's no better or worse person than any other person. And they should be given the most opportunities from their schooling to help them determine where their own personal directions are. It's not like the old system where they're graded. They're not a percentage, they're human beings. They are catered for. The individualness comes out and is promoted.*

Elements deduced from the primary data

- valuing of each individual student;
- belief in maximum opportunities for all students;
- curriculum which caters for all students and their needs

Leads to the hypothesized symbolic student outcome

A belief in the intrinsic value of each student ⇒ student self-worth ⇒ climate conducive to learning ⇒ development of student potential.

The significance of such connections is in *tracking* the consequences of the action being taken, because from this, predictable patterns of responses emerge. Once these patterns become entrenched they determine the school culture, and knowing what they are likely to be means that leaders can, to a large extent, direct and develop the culture. That is, patterns of responsive behaviour lead to *norms* of behaviour which bring positive consequences in terms of structural, human resource, political and symbolic outcomes. Further, one action may set off a variety of responses and produce multiple outcomes. Leader action can therefore be surprisingly economical if efforts are focused and pin-point the desired purpose.

The following section looks at the connections observed from collaborative leader action taken in the five schools investigated in inner city Melbourne, and the positive implications which these actions incurred for students, staff and the school.

Hypothesized Causal Links Between the Structural Frame and School Success – Student, Teacher and Organizational Outcomes

Student Outcomes – Structural Frame

- Student-focused staff meetings ⇒ individualized curriculum ⇒ climate conducive to learning ⇒ development of educational potential;
- Student-focused staff meetings ⇒ individualized student pastoral care ⇒ positive student behaviour ⇒ development of educational potential;
- Whole staff decision-making ⇒ combined staff action ⇒ consistency of approach ⇒ clear expectations ⇒ positive student behaviour;
- Whole staff decision-making ⇒ innovative curriculum ⇒ development of educational potential;
- Whole staff decision-making ⇒ clarity of teaching purposes ⇒ climate conducive to learning ⇒ engagement in learning;
- Leadership density ⇒ student empowerment ⇒ a climate conducive to learning ⇒ development of educational potential;
- Leadership density ⇒ student empowerment ⇒ self determination.

Here three structural factors contribute directly to positive student outcomes – student-focused staff meetings, whole staff decision-making and leadership density. By instigating these three structural arrangements, student outcomes of the development of educational potential, positive behaviour, engagement in learning, and self-determination are achieved.

In the case of student-focused staff meetings, the individualized understanding and care of students is influential in developing positive behaviour and attitudes to learning. Knowing each student enables this individualized approach, is gained through staff time *expended on the needs of students*, both social and academic, in routine staff meetings. This is in direct contrast to a focus on administrative procedures.

Whole-staff decision-making results in similar student outcomes, including an engagement in learning. Combined staff action leads to a consistency of approach which gives clear expectations to students across all subjects and year levels resulting in good student behaviour. United action on the part of teachers in terms of innovative curriculum development, leads to learning activities and a teaching/learning environment which caters to the particular demands of the student clientele, not to the level of the hypothetical average student. This, in turn, encourages students to take a positive view of themselves as learners, provides a climate conducive to learning and to the development of their educational potential.

Commitment to the concept of leadership density allows for real student empowerment. Students have a say in their immediate future as far as school is concerned, for example, in the way play space is organized or in influencing decisions about camps or excursions. Any concerns students may have can be addressed through a formal process which legitimizes student participation in decision-making. Valuing students' ideas and suggestions, and providing a spirit of cooperation between staff and students, engenders a climate conducive to learning, resulting in the development of educational potential and a genuine feeling in each student that they can really make things happen if they want to. This is a considerable achievement given the complex nature of the student clientele, many of whom come from backgrounds which do not lend themselves to active participation in formal decision-making processes either in the educational or broader societal context.

Collaborative structural leadership effects:

- a central focus of using school structures to address and support students' learning;
- development of educational potential;
- engagement in learning;
- positive student behaviour;
- self-determination.

Just as collaborative structural arrangements bring accomplishment for students, so, too, can they bring successful outcomes for teachers in schools. The following connections have been made between effective structural leadership and teacher success.

Teacher Outcomes – Structural Frame

- Democratic processes $\Rightarrow$ staff cooperation $\Rightarrow$ cohesive staff $\Rightarrow$ high morale $\Rightarrow$ love of teaching;
- Democratic processes $\Rightarrow$ power of individual to make change $\Rightarrow$ high staff morale $\Rightarrow$ sense of professional satisfaction;
- Democratic meeting procedures $\Rightarrow$ opportunities for increasing teacher skills $\Rightarrow$ professional development;
- Democratic selection of roles $\Rightarrow$ equitable, merit-based appointments $\Rightarrow$ professional respect of leaders $\Rightarrow$ harmonious staff relationships;
- Democratic selection of roles $\Rightarrow$ equitable, merit-based appointments $\Rightarrow$ opportunities for broad ranging professional development.

Democratic processes, including democratic meeting procedures and selection of roles, play an important part in bringing about success for teachers in schools. When the decision-making process cultivates widespread consultation and discussion, decisions are reached with full knowledge of staff concerning both the issues involved and the reasons for the decision. Teachers know they have had a fair say in the arguments put forward and, as such, are likely to cooperate in the implementation of the decision. The processes which give individual teachers the power to make change, leads to staff norms of high morale and a sense of professional satisfaction.

Democratic meeting procedures such as rotation of the Chair and minute-taking, having an open agenda and assisting all staff to become familiar with formal meeting procedures, give opportunities for all teachers to take part in the formal processes of the school and in so doing, increase their professional skills. Democratic processes in the selection of senior staff positions allow for responsibility to be held by those with the particular skills required at the time, rather than on the basis of seniority. This avoids the ownership of positions of responsibility and not only has the effect of the getting the best person for the job, but also opens up career opportunities to all members of the staff regardless of their years of experience, leading to the opportunity for broad-ranging professional development. Voting by colleagues (rather than the formal hierarchy) determines the appointment. The consequence of this approach is equitable, merit-based appointments, professional respect by teachers for their leaders and harmonious staff relationships.

Effective structural leadership brings about teacher outcomes of:

- a strongly committed and supportive staff;
- broad-ranging professional development;
- high teacher morale;
- high level of teacher involvement;
- a love of teaching.

Great professional benefits to teachers result as a consequence of democratic procedures operating in schools. Similarly, there are repercussions for organizational outcomes from the structural perspective.

Organizational Outcomes – Structural Frame

- Vision ⇒ clarity of purpose ⇒ technical culture;
- Openness in procedures and processes ⇒ trust and belief in democratic process ⇒ confidence in decisions ⇒ strong involvement and commitment;
- Democratic structures ⇒ leadership density ⇒ staff commitment ⇒ institutionalization of vision;
- Democratic processes ⇒ a sense of fairness and equity ⇒ acceptance of majority decision ⇒ cooperation and support by all sectors of the school community;
- Democratic processes ⇒ leadership density ⇒ shared decision-making ⇒ maximum pool of skills/talents ⇒ well-understood, quality decisions;
- Democratic structures ⇒ constant flow of information ⇒ sound communication;

- Democratic organization ⇒ leadership density ⇒ effective whole school planning and implementation;
- Democratic selection of roles ⇒ staff commitment ⇒ effectiveness.

Clear vision brings clarity of purpose, and, this in turn ensures that the vision translates into a technical culture. In other words, the vision constantly directs the school's varied activity to the central focus of teaching and learning, and the structural arrangements of the school are deliberately organized to support this. The organization then is able to fulfil its central task – to enhance student achievement.

Openness in procedures and processes centres around an open-door policy which invites and promotes all people to show expressions of interest in school decision-making. Democratic processes also promote a sense of fairness and equity which facilitate the acceptance of majority decisions. Trust and belief in democratic process follow, resulting in a corporate confidence in organizational decisions. The knowledge that decisions have been arrived at in a fair and equitable way form a strong base for cooperation, support, involvement and commitment of all members of the school community.

Democratic structure is characterized by an absence of structural hierarchy and autocratic decision-making. This enables leadership density with widespread empowerment, as well as representation of all sectors of the school community. What ensues is a firm commitment to the implementation of the organizational vision which is grounded in the routine activities of the school. In addition, leadership density, facilitated by democratic processes, provides the means for shared decision-making. This, in turn, paves the way for the maximum pool of skills and talents to be utilized and fed into the decision-making process, with resultant sound, well-understood, quality decisions.

A constant flow of information throughout all sectors of the school community is provided by the wide representation of democratic structures. Freely shared information from open forums, and access to written material (such as minutes of meetings and drafts of changing school policies) leads to sound communication, which produces effective whole school planning. Democratic selection of roles give encouragement to all to take on positions of responsibility, especially when accompanied by strong informal and formal support. This creates staff commitment and brings about school effectiveness.

In terms of organizational success, a combination of the above structural leadership action brings about:

- a technical culture;
- strong involvement and commitment;
- institutionalization of vision;
- co-operation and support by all sectors of the school community;
- well-understood, quality decisions;
- efficient operating of the school through effective planning;
- trust and confidence in the decision-making process;
- clear communication and guidelines.

Leaders in the participating schools should be cognisant of the formal structure and operations of the school embodied in the structural frame, knowing that school success can be achieved when goals are clear and infused into daily activities through sound communication, clearly understood democratic decision-making processes, and well organized and well run meetings. Individual efforts can be directed by formal procedures which guide policies and rules and institutionalize the vision of the school. Great store should be put in everyone having a 'fair go' and sharing roles of responsibility for the health of the school. Democratic processes play a particularly significant role in achieving success in schools, as does the underlying belief of leaders that all children should have full educational opportunities and that school arrangements can make this happen. A valuing of interpersonal openness also contributes to a collaborative culture in the schools and to their success.

Hypothesized Causal Links Between the Findings of the Human Resource Frame and School Success – Student, Teacher and Organizational Outcomes

Student Outcomes – Human Resource Frame

- Commonly held educational philosophy ⇒ cooperative planning/evaluation ⇒ consistent monitoring of programs ⇒ a constantly developing curriculum ⇒ engagement in learning;
- Organizational fit ⇒ professional satisfaction ⇒ continuous teacher learning ⇒ innovative curriculum ⇒ climate conducive to learning;
- Professional honesty ⇒ sharing of successes/failures ⇒ continuous teacher learning ⇒ development of educational potential for students;
- Organizational fit ⇒ high morale ⇒ love of teaching ⇒ enthusiastic teachers ⇒ climate conducive to learning ⇒ an engagement in learning;
- Task-focused teachers ⇒ teamwork ⇒ cooperative attention to student needs ⇒ student social and academic support ⇒ positive student behaviour;
- Student-based school culture ⇒ good student/staff relationships ⇒ positive student behaviour.

Teachers who have a commonly held educational philosophy combine successfully in their professional work, to jointly undertake cooperative planning and evaluation of teaching and learning activities. This means that consistent monitoring of programs and a constantly developing curriculum occur. A base of educational activity which caters to the needs of students results in engagement in learning. In addition, organizational fit leads to high morale and a love of teaching. Enthusiastic teachers promote a climate conducive to learning and, once again, result in an engagement in learning for students.

Organizational fit occurs when the needs of the organization and those of individual staff members are mutually satisfied. In the case of establishing and sustaining a technical culture, organizational fit is dependent on encouraging all staff to express their professional individuality and particular fortes in the planning of curriculum. Giving teachers such professional opportunity generates professional satisfaction, which returns to the organization a culture of continuous teacher learning. An innovative curriculum results with the outcome for students being a climate conducive to learning.

When an atmosphere of openness and a sense of common responsibility for students is instituted, staff feel comfortable to discuss their uncertainties and seek shared solutions to concerns or problems. This has the repercussion of developing professional honesty, where sharing of successes and failures can readily take place. The consequence of this professional sharing is continuous teacher learning which, in turn, brings about the development of educational opportunities for students.

Teachers who can put aside personality differences to focus on the task at hand operate on the understanding that the interests of the students override the idiosyncrasies of individual staff members. Task-focused teamwork initiates cooperative attention to student needs. This focus instigates social and academic support for students and activates positive student behaviour. Moreover, a student-based school culture promotes good student/staff relationships which, again, promote positive student behaviour.

The specific human resource leadership behaviour discussed above can create conditions for educational success for students. These outcomes are as follows:

- climate conducive to learning;
- engagement in learning;
- development of educational potential for students;
- positive student behaviour.

Teacher Outcomes – Human Resource Frame

- Organizational fit $\Rightarrow$ professional confidence $\Rightarrow$ positive mood/high morale $\Rightarrow$ professional development/continuous learning $\Rightarrow$ increased teacher skills;
- Organizational fit $\Rightarrow$ personal/professional expression $\Rightarrow$ stimulating practice $\Rightarrow$ high morale $\Rightarrow$ love of teaching;
- Mutual respect and acceptance $\Rightarrow$ cooperative teacher learning $\Rightarrow$ professional stimulation $\Rightarrow$ on-going school-based professional development;
- Formal/informal support $\Rightarrow$ staff cohesiveness/camaraderie $\Rightarrow$ high morale;

- Team planning/support ⇒ shared responsibility/workload ⇒ professional development.

Organizational fit brings twofold benefits to teachers in schools. It leads directly to personal and professional expression which creates a climate for stimulating practice, resulting in high morale and a love of teaching. It also serves to build professional confidence which leads to a positive mood, which encourages professional development and continuous learning by teachers. High morale is produced by staff cohesiveness, and a sense of camaraderie is brought about through formal and informal support. Leaders can establish a formal expectation that staff will help each other, giving approval to an informal *and* a formal, network of support. This can be achieved through a great deal of informal reinforcing talk, and by encouraging a working environment of mutual support, professional acceptance and continuous learning. Mutual respect and acceptance by colleagues instigate cooperative teacher learning. Cooperative teacher-learning fosters professional stimulation, which leads to on-going school-based professional development. Professional development is similarly generated by team planning and support and the comfort of shared responsibility and workload.

Effective human resource leadership brings about the following outcomes for teachers:

- a stimulating professional atmosphere;
- continuous learning;
- increased teacher skills;
- love of teaching;
- high teacher morale;
- a cohesive staff group;
- a formal and informal support network.

Organizational Outcomes – Human Resource Frame

- Organizational fit ⇒ cooperation/commitment ⇒ institutionalization of vision;
- Organizational fit ⇒ personal/professional expression ⇒ stimulating practice ⇒ love of teaching ⇒ sustaining technical culture;
- Organizational fit ⇒ personal/professional satisfaction ⇒ high morale ⇒ sound organizational health;
- Organizational fit ⇒ personal/professional expression ⇒ stimulating practice ⇒ high morale ⇒ hard work/commitment;
- Formal/informal support ⇒ cooperation/commitment ⇒ institutionalization of vision/sound organizational health;
- Staff-centred administrative arrangements ⇒ opportunities to operate cooperatively ⇒ team approach ⇒ effective management;

- Mutual respect and acceptance ⇒ cooperative teacher learning ⇒ sustaining culture of continuous teacher learning.

Human resource leadership should make a concerted attempt to match the needs of individuals with the needs of the school as an organizational whole. In this way the full potential and abilities of school community members will be realized, and their collective capacities will form the driving force behind achieving the educational vision and goals of the school. Leaders in schools who seek out the skills and talents of school community members and match these to roles and responsibilities assist in achieving organizational fit. Similarly, leaders who respond to the needs of individuals and align these appropriately with roles and responsibilities in their school, will generate cooperation and commitment, which, in turn, grounds the vision into daily practice. As well, organizational fit allows for professional expression and satisfaction, which cultivates stimulating practice, resulting in a love of teaching and the sustaining of a technical culture. Personal and professional satisfaction also breeds high morale, which motivates hard work and commitment, and is directly responsible for sound organizational health. Staff-centred administrative arrangements give opportunities to operate cooperatively, effecting a team approach which produces effective management. Mutual respect and acceptance, characterized by leaders who have a deep-seated belief in the intrinsic value of each individual member of staff, give opportunities for cooperative teacher learning, which respectively sustains a culture of continuous teacher learning. As a result, human resource leadership can produce organizational outcomes of:

- institutionalization of vision;
- sustaining technical culture;
- sound organizational health;
- hard work/commitment;
- effective management;
- continuous teacher learning.

Through the human resource frame, leaders can bring success for their students, staff and school, by focusing on the needs and skills of the people in the organization. Students must be a primary focus, with emphasis being given to serving the social welfare needs of students as well as their educational ones. Curriculum can be designed to cater to the particular needs of students and will be generally innovative as a result, and at the cutting edge of professional practice. In addition to student needs, teachers' professional needs should be given a high priority, knowing that teachers are able to work best when their professional needs are met, and when they have support and encouragement to develop as competent and valued staff members. An open-door policy encourages parents to be actively involved. Schools can gauge their success against the extent to which they respond to the needs of their diverse school communities, and have the capacity to bring everyone together in a spirit of sharing and harmony.

Hypothesized Causal Links Between the Findings of the Political Frame and School Success – Student, Teacher and Organizational Outcomes

Student Outcomes – Political Frame:

- Promotion of democratic processes $\Rightarrow$ wide representation $\Rightarrow$ sharing of power $\Rightarrow$ a sense of empowerment $\Rightarrow$ positive behaviour;
- Promotion of democratic processes $\Rightarrow$ wide representation $\Rightarrow$ sharing of power $\Rightarrow$ participation in, and experience of, the democratic process;
- Promotion of democratic processes $\Rightarrow$ wide representation $\Rightarrow$ leadership responsibility;
- Promotion of democratic processes $\Rightarrow$ opportunities to express personal opinions $\Rightarrow$ personal growth;
- Promotion of democratic processes $\Rightarrow$ opportunities to share the ideas of others $\Rightarrow$ development of cooperative learning skills;
- Open, honest communication $\Rightarrow$ respect for and valuing of others' point of view $\Rightarrow$ sharing of ideas $\Rightarrow$ shared problem-solving $\Rightarrow$ innovation in the curriculum;
- Agreed-upon political behaviour $\Rightarrow$ creation of coalitions based on issues (rather than personalities) $\Rightarrow$ positive political influence $\Rightarrow$ harmonious learning environment.

Leaders who promote democratic processes create significant and multiple outcomes for students in their schools. Wide representation through participatory processes institutes the sharing of power and leads to a sense of empowerment in students, which results in positive behaviour. Wide representation and the sharing of power also enable participation in, and experience of, the democratic process and can bring leadership responsibility. Promotion of democratic processes fosters opportunities to express personal opinions and to facilitate personal growth. It also provides opportunities to share the ideas of others and contributes to the development of cooperative learning skills. Open, honest communication develops a climate of trust and encourages staff to express their opinions freely, leading to an environment where problems are shared and solved with colleagues. In fostering active participation by all sections of the school community in the decision-making processes, leaders should identify agreed-upon political behaviour, including the creation of coalitions based on issues (rather than personalities). This brings about positive political influence, which leads to a harmonious learning environment.

So, politically astute leadership results in the following outcomes for students:

- positive behaviour;
- participation in, and experience of, the democratic process;
- leadership responsibility;
- personal growth;

- development of cooperative learning skills;
- innovation in the curriculum;
- harmonious learning environment.

Teacher Outcomes – Political Frame

- Agreed-upon political behaviour ⇒ disagreements not seen as disrupt-ive ⇒ diffusion of conflict -⇒ harmonious working relationships;
- Agreed-upon political behaviour ⇒ disagreements not seen as disrupt-ive ⇒ diffusion of conflict ⇒ staff cohesion ⇒ high morale ⇒ staff commitment/enthusiasm;
- Promotion of democratic processes ⇒ wide representation ⇒ sharing of authority ⇒ shared responsibility ⇒ professional satisfaction;
- Promotion of democratic processes ⇒ wide representation ⇒ oppor-tunities to express opinions ⇒ harmonious working atmosphere;
- Fair and equitable decision-making ⇒ agreement via consensus/vote ⇒ acceptance of decisions ⇒ lack of dissension ⇒ harmony;
- Fair and equitable decision-making ⇒ agreement via consensus/ vote ⇒ acceptance of decisions ⇒ staff cohesion ⇒ high morale/job satisfaction;
- Open, honest communication ⇒ respect for and valuing of others' point of view ⇒ sharing of ideas ⇒ informed decisions/professional stimulation;
- Information accessible to all ⇒ trust in the processes ⇒ harmony ⇒ cohesive staff;
- Accessibility ⇒ of information/forums ⇒ opportunity for negotiation/ compromise ⇒ sense of trust ⇒ satisfaction that the system is fair ⇒ high morale/professional satisfaction.

Leaders in schools see political processes as part of everyday school life and exert a positive influence in an informal way by lobbying for outcomes which will advance the educational agenda. Agreed-upon political behaviour accepts that disagreements are inevitable and are not seen as disruptive. This leads to diffusion of conflict and creates more harmonious working relationships. Similarly, agreed-upon political behaviour where disagreements are not seen as disruptive, diffuses conflict, leading to staff cohesion, high morale, and staff commitment/enthusiasm follows.

Promotion of democratic processes has the effect of sharing of authority through widespread representation which provides the means for shared responsibility and ensuing professional satisfaction. Promotion of democratic processes furthers opportunities to express opinions which gives rise to a harmonious working atmosphere. Based on a satisfaction that the system is fair, decision-making facilitates agreement being reached via consensus or majority vote. This consultative process leads to an acceptance of decisions, a lack of dissension and resulting harmony. As well, where there is acceptance of decisions on the basis of fair and equitable decision-making, staff cohesion is strong and high morale and job satisfaction result.

Leaders can lead by example in modelling an openness and honesty in presenting points of view. Open, honest communication which respects, and values others' points of view, provides for the sharing of ideas, which leads to informed decisions and ensuing professional stimulation.

Leaders who ensure all information is accessible to all build trust in the decision-making processes. Trust gives rise to harmony and the creation of a cohesive staff. Accessibility of information through open meetings or forums maximizes the opportunity for negotiation and compromise *before* decisions are reached, developing a sense of trust and a satisfaction that the system is fair. High morale and professional satisfaction flourish under these conditions.

Teacher outcomes of effective political leadership are:

- harmonious working relationships;
- staff commitment/enthusiasm;
- professional satisfaction;
- high morale/job satisfaction;
- professional stimulation;
- cohesive staff.

Organizational Outcomes – Political Frame

- Acceptance of politics as routine $\Rightarrow$ problems/conflict seen as inevitable $\Rightarrow$ development of formal political processes $\Rightarrow$ sense of trust $\Rightarrow$ good organizational health;
- Awareness of the informal political network $\Rightarrow$ opportunity for diffusion of conflict $\Rightarrow$ good organizational health;
- Promotion of democratic processes $\Rightarrow$ wide representation $\Rightarrow$ well thought through decisions;
- Promotion of democratic processes $\Rightarrow$ wide representation $\Rightarrow$ strong communication;
- Promotion of democratic processes $\Rightarrow$ wide representation $\Rightarrow$ greater coordination/planning;
- Fair and equitable decision-making $\Rightarrow$ acceptance of decisions $\Rightarrow$ strong commitment to the implementation of decisions;
- Creation of open forums for discussion $\Rightarrow$ public defence of views $\Rightarrow$ open, honest communication $\Rightarrow$ avoidance of self-interest $\Rightarrow$ satisfaction that the system is fair $\Rightarrow$ good organizational health.

Leaders who hold the belief that politics in the school is routine, see problems or conflict as inescapable. In order to address problems or conflicts at the school level, formal political processes which are clearly understood to all are put into place to ensure a just resolution is achieved. Trust in the administrative procedures eventuates, and good organizational health ensues. In addition, astute political leaders take careful account of the informal politics in the organization and seize the opportunity to negotiate the underground political network to diffuse conflict to bring about good organizational health.

Promotion of democratic processes in the political arena has a threefold effect. Through widespread representation it brings about well thought through decisions, strong communication and greater coordination and planning.

Open forums, where points of view are defended publicly, avoid self-interest and negative manipulation of the decision-making process. Accordingly, fair and equitable decision-making takes place, with a resulting acceptance of decisions. What follows as a consequence, is a strong commitment to the implementation of decisions, a satisfaction that the system is fair and good organizational health.

Effective political leadership brings about significant outcomes for the school:

- good organizational health;
- well thought through decisions;
- strong communication;
- greater coordination and planning;
- a stronger commitment by staff, student and parents to the implementation of decisions.

Focusing on the political frame, leaders recognize the need to concentrate on political relations and how they operate in the school, displaying a willingness to face and deal with conflicts and deliberately exercise their moral authority to stand up for, and take action over, what they believe in, when competing or conflicting values presented themselves in the school community. Democratic processes are held dear in achieving fair and just outcomes, and leaders promote empowerment and active participation across the school community. Legitimate political behaviour is supported through fair and equitable school-based procedures, decisions being reached by consensus or majority vote. Attitudes of egalitarianism, inclusiveness and openness prevail, furthering the development of a collaborative culture, which, in turn, brings success to the schools in terms of a cohesive community characterized by positive relations and facilitation of a strong focus on teaching and learning.

Hypothesized Causal Links Between the Symbolic Frame and School Success – Student, Teacher and Organizational Outcomes

Student Outcomes – Symbolic Frame

- a belief that disadvantaged children should have full educational opportunities $\Rightarrow$ special school arrangements $\Rightarrow$ social welfare support programs $\Rightarrow$ development of educational potential;

- an attitude of caring and respect by staff ⇒ modelling of norms of behaviour ⇒ an attitude of caring and respect in students;
- an attitude of acceptance of differences ⇒ modelling of norms of behaviour ⇒ a student attitude of acceptance of differences;
- a belief in the intrinsic value of each individual student ⇒ student self-worth ⇒ climate conducive to learning ⇒ development of student potential;
- valuing of diversity ⇒ acceptance of differences ⇒ an absence of racial tension ⇒ climate conducive to learning;
- value of interpersonal openness ⇒ egalitarian approach by staff ⇒ mutual acceptance and respect ⇒ climate conducive to learning ⇒ engagement in learning.

When there is a strongly held belief that disadvantaged children should have full educational opportunities, people in schools will put into place special school arrangements to make this happen. Such arrangements often take the form of social welfare support programs, for many students in inner city schools are troubled with social and emotional needs which must necessarily take priority over educational ones. Children who are hungry or homeless, for instance, are unlikely to embrace the complexities of learning until the urgency of their immediate physical and emotional concerns are met. If schools are prepared to take on a social welfare role, they are more likely to keep these students in the school, and thereby provide opportunities for the development of their educational potential. Modelling by staff of care and respect for students leads to norms of behaviour in the school which develop an attitude of caring and respect in students themselves. The same goes for an attitude of acceptance of differences, where once again, modelling by teachers and others in the school community engenders a student culture where an attitude of acceptance of differences becomes the norm.

Closely aligned to acceptance of difference is a fundamental belief in the intrinsic value of each individual student. Valuing the individual leads to student self-worth. Students who have high self-esteem are able to see themselves as successful learners and this develops their educational potential. Valuing of interpersonal openness means that an egalitarian approach is adopted by staff, creating a relationship between teachers and students of mutual acceptance and respect, which in turn, effects a climate conducive to learning and engagement in learning by students.

Valuing diversity leads to acceptance of differences, which directly results in an absence of racial tension. In a multicultural school setting where many cultural groups are living and learning under the one roof this is a highly desirable outcome, as the harmonious environment which emanates from a valuing of diversity provides a climate which can focus directly on learning, rather than having to deal with negative behaviour associated with racism.

Overall, there is a significant connection between the values and attitudes demonstrated in the school and student success. Resulting outcomes for students are listed below:

- development for educational potential;
- an attitude of caring and respect by students;
- a student attitude of acceptance of differences;
- a climate conducive to learning;
- an engagement in learning.

Teacher Outcomes – Symbolic Frame

- a shared belief that disadvantaged children should have full educational opportunities ⇒ combined staff action ⇒ high staff morale/job satisfaction;
- a belief in the intrinsic value of each individual member of staff ⇒ mutual support and respect ⇒ high morale ⇒ love of teaching;
- valuing of diversity ⇒ acceptance of differences expressing of individuality ⇒ satisfaction of needs;
- value of interpersonal openness ⇒ staff interaction ⇒ reinforcement of beliefs and values ⇒ sustaining of a collaborative staff culture;
- valuing of diversity ⇒ acceptance of differences ⇒ an absence of racial tension ⇒ harmonious working relationships.

Teachers who share a belief that disadvantaged children should have full educational opportunities can collectively take staff action to implement their belief in practice. In achieving their goal, high staff morale results and job satisfaction ensues. A belief in the intrinsic value of each individual member of staff brings mutual support and respect, again producing high morale, which in turn effects a love of teaching. Valuing of diversity brings an acceptance of differences, which allows expression of individuality, with the outcome of satisfying professional needs. Interpersonal openness fosters staff interaction, providing reinforcement of shared beliefs and values, and this results in the sustaining of a collaborative staff culture. Valuing of diversity in both staff and students leads to a school culture which accepts difference. This leads to harmonious working relationships void of racial tension.

Causal connections of the symbolic frame clearly bring success for teachers. They are as follows:

- high staff morale;
- job satisfaction;
- love of teaching;
- satisfaction of needs;
- sustaining of a collaborative staff culture;
- harmonious working relationships.

Organizational Outcomes – Symbolic Frame

- a belief that disadvantaged children should have full educational opportunities ⇒ extensive educational support ⇒ cooperative team approach ⇒ institutionalization of vision;
- an attitude of caring and respect by staff ⇒ modelling of norms of behaviour ⇒ an attitude of caring and respect in whole school community ⇒ institutionalization of values and beliefs ⇒ sustaining of collaborative culture;
- an attitude of caring and respect by staff ⇒ modelling of norms of behaviour ⇒ an attitude of caring and respect in whole school community;
- a belief that disadvantaged children should have full educational opportunities ⇒ special school arrangements ⇒ social welfare support programs ⇒ sound organizational health;
- value of interpersonal openness ⇒ egalitarian approach by staff ⇒ mutual acceptance and respect ⇒ cohesive staff/student/parent community;
- value of interpersonal openness ⇒ interaction/socializing ⇒ reinforcement of shared beliefs/values ⇒ institutionalization of vision;
- Symbols/rituals/ceremonies ⇒ reinforcement of shared beliefs/values ⇒ institutionalization of vision.

Institutionalization of vision refers here to the ability of leaders to organize and operate their schools in such a way that strongly held values and beliefs are reflected in the day to day pursuits of the school. In other words, practising what you preach becomes the norm. So often in schools the rhetoric is understood, accepted and even articulated, but there is a notable absence of it in reality. Institutionalization of vision is the leadership capacity to firmly establish *vision in practice*, making the critical difference to achieving school success.

In the project schools the predominant driving tenet was that disadvantaged children should have full educational opportunities. This belief leads to two distinct outcomes as far as the organization is concerned – institutionalization of vision and sound organizational health. Holding the belief that disadvantaged children should have full educational opportunities leads to the provision of extensive educational support. This generates a cooperative team approach with staff working closely together as a team in the interests of the students, which in turn translates the vision into practice. As well, this belief safeguards the needs of disadvantaged students by making special school arrangements through social welfare support programs. With the social welfare of needs of students attended to, teachers, as well as students, are better able to get on with the primary purposes of teaching and learning leading to sound organizational health.

Modelling an attitude of caring and respect by staff leads to norms of behaviour in which there is caring and respect for all members of the school community. It also brings about the institutionalization of values and beliefs which sustain a collaborative culture. This may take the form of interpersonal openness where an egalitarian approach by staff leads to mutual acceptance and respect of all school community members, resulting in a cohesive staff, student and parent community. Valuing interpersonal openness promotes interaction and socializing, which has the consequence of reinforcing shared beliefs and values, which once again produces institutionalization of vision. Symbols, rituals and ceremonies which are carefully orchestrated by school leaders reinforce shared beliefs and values and also positively impacting on the institutionalizing of the vision of the school.

In various connections and cross connections symbolic elements lead to the following successful outcomes for the school as an organization:

- institutionalization of vision;
- sustaining of collaborative culture;
- an attitude of caring and respect in whole school community;
- sound organizational health;
- cohesive staff/student/parent community.

Leaders attaining success for their schools work through the symbolic frame of the organizational life of the school, knowing that students, teachers and parents are significantly influenced by the beliefs, values, routines and conventions, explicit or implicit, in the practice of school activities. The symbolic frame is immersed in beliefs, values, attitudes and norms of behaviour, which are represented through symbols, rituals and ceremonies and are interwoven through the structural, human resource and political frames. In school communities, specific beliefs, values, attitudes and norms of behaviour are fervently held by the majority of leaders. Fundamental to the leaders' behaviour and endeavours, are the identification of those beliefs, in the case of this study it was a belief that disadvantaged children should have full educational opportunities and that school arrangements can make this happen. There was also a further belief in the intrinsic value of each individual – student, staff member or parent. A valuing of diversity, an acceptance of differences and a regard for interpersonal openness permeate the attitudes of people in the schools in this investigation. Success is achieved by effectively reacting to the distinctive social and educational needs of their urban clientele, providing students with optimum opportunities to gain personal choice and fulfilment in their adult lives.

Summary

The linking process of cause and effect is a valuable one. It extricates very specific features from the concentrated richness of each frame, and, importantly, allows pathways to be constructed which follow a route created by each foregoing factor. Each step along the way is initiated by its predecessor, often with different paths verging off from the same beginnings, providing multiple outcomes from one source. This has deep significance for leaders in schools, for it means that there is a certain predictability within the irrationality of organizational life, which can be tapped to bring a degree of success to students, teachers and the organization.

Collaborative Leadership

During the process of specifically identifying the *hypothesized* causal links leading to student, teacher and organizational success, it became apparent that other configurations of relationships might be occurring. Consequently, a synthesis of the hypothesized causal links was undertaken *outside* the four frames. Each hypothesized causal link was individually sorted, disregarding the frames, into several emerging but distinct patterns. A distillation of the causal links was thus effected, bringing valuable insights as to what it is that constitutes the *heart* of the collaborative milieu, and what it is in *essence* that brings about school success. Four dominant factors (outside the Bolman and Deal typology) were apparent. They are as follows:

- development of the educational potential of students;
- professional development of teachers;
- good organizational health;
- institutionalization of vision.

These four critical factors form a synthesis of the sum and substance of the hypothesized causal links and are summarized below.

Development of the Educational Potential of Students

The developing of educational potential for students centres around three core factors – positive student behaviour, a climate conducive to learning and an innovative curriculum designed to meet student needs. Positive behaviour includes caring and respect for fellow students, a student attitude of acceptance of differences and a developing of cooperative learning skills such as listening to and respecting the opinions of others. These attitudes and skills have direct implications for positive discipline in the school, where, together with consistent expectations from staff, cooperation is encouraged and unacceptable behaviour which might disrupt or inhibit learning is minimized. Moreover, empowerment of students brings opportunities for personal growth and leadership responsibility, as well as for choice in the curriculum, which in turn facilitate engagement in learning.

Closely aligned to positive student behaviour is the development of a climate conducive to learning, where open and approachable relationships between staff and students lead to mutual acceptance and respect. A belief in the intrinsic value of each student produces a feeling of self-worth, a positive approach to learning and a development of educational potential. As well special school arrangements such as social welfare and support programs advance the academic learning environment for students in urban schools.

An innovative curriculum which is constantly developing clarity of teaching purposes, cooperative curriculum planning and evaluation all contribute to meeting the individual needs of students. Student-focused staff meetings play an important role in catering for students whether it be with regard to individualized pastoral care or individualized curriculum.

Thus, positive student behaviour, a climate conducive to learning and an innovative curriculum designed to meet student needs all play a critical role in developing the educational potential of urban students.

Professional Development of Teachers

Organizational fit, continuous teacher learning, and professional satisfaction and a love of teaching have direct impact on the professional development of teachers. Organizational fit allows for personal and professional expression which brings about professional stimulation and satisfaction. In addition, a belief in the intrinsic value of each individual staff member leads to mutual support and respect. This flows on to continuous teacher learning which is achieved through teacher empowerment, shared responsibility, cooperative planning and the sharing of ideas. Both organizational fit and continuous teacher learning jointly lead to professional satisfaction and a love of teaching. This, in conjunction with democratic, merit-based appointments, enhances the professional development of teachers.

Good Organizational Health

Good organizational health is generated via a technical culture, harmonious relationships and effective management. Technical culture refers to the organizational focus of teaching and learning as the school's *raison d'etre*, bringing clarity of purpose and a clear direction to the operation of the school. Harmonious relationships across the school community cultivate a cordial, congenial and supportive working environment for students, staff and school community members, producing cohesion and high morale. Effective management leads to well-understood, quality decisions, strong communication, and whole school coordination and planning. Together, a technical culture, harmonious relationships and effective management provide the key ingredients in creating good organizational health.

Institutionalization of Vision

Shared beliefs, leadership density, and commitment, cooperation and support are pivotal to the institutionalization of vision. Beliefs which are shared bring a common purpose and underpinning of the daily practices of the school. Moreover, if these shared beliefs are accompanied by shared power and bona fide responsibility, a spread of leadership saturates the organization so that leaders across many roles are committed to implementing the shared purposes or vision. It is not sufficient, in achieving success in schools, to have shared vision without the accompanying depth of leadership necessary to translate it into practice. Leadership density with its breadth of leadership and wide representation enables a collective reinforcing of the guiding values and attitudes of the school. When beliefs are shared amongst the members of the school community, and when a density of leadership is present, then the vision of the school is poised to become institutionalized. Significantly however, for institutionalization of vision to occur, cooperation, support and commitment must accompany shared beliefs and leadership density.

In the process of isolating these four fundamental understandings from the aggregated hypothesized causal connections, it becomes clear that each of the four is intimately related to each other and the connections and cross connections between them appear limitless. For example, harmonious relationships are interrelated to positive student behaviour and to cooperation and support, and to professional satisfaction; innovation in the curriculum is interdependent with continuous teacher learning and a technical culture; and high morale is entwined with a climate conducive to learning and to cooperation and commitment. What is of significance here is that the four demonstrable outcomes which generate a collaborative culture are *inextricably linked and interdependent*. It could be said, therefore, that where *all* four outcomes are present and operate simultaneously, a fully functioning collaborative culture has been established.

Chapter 9

Issues and Reflections

Leaders and Collaborative Cultures

Leaders are able to achieve success in their schools when they can simultaneously comprehend, interpret and capitalize on four frames of reference – structural, human resource, political and symbolic (Bolman and Deal, 1991), drawing on the particular insights and understandings which each conveys. Unlike the view of some writers (Johnson, 1990; Schein, 1985), the position taken in this book is that leadership forces of a school culture are not restricted to the symbolic dimension *alone*. 'Culture' as it is defined here, embraces the four overarching perspectives of structural, human resource, political and symbolic dimensions. All have influence, all have commensurate insights to bring to bear, all are equivalent parts which collectively complete the whole.

Susan Moore Johnson (1990:218) argues that preference should be given to shaping cultural bonds ('symbolic aspects of shared purposes, values, traditions and history') over 'rational bonds' ('rules, roles, functions, penalties and formal authority that specify and regulate the behaviour of individuals in organizations') if schools are to be effective. Her argument gives strong preference to the symbolic aspects of leadership, over the structural ones. Both Schein and Johnson seem to be suggesting that symbolic aspects should take on a higher priority and prominence, or somehow be favoured over other leadership forces. In Johnson's case, this view is based on the premise that 'rational bonds . . . presume reluctance and dissent rather than commitment and accord.' The findings of the structural frame presented in this book would suggest otherwise (Page 55). Contrary to attitudes of reluctance and dissent, causal linkages between the structural frame and school success are characterized by high morale, staff commitment, active participation, cooperation and support by all sectors of the school community. Schein appears to be arguing that symbolic aspects are such powerful forces, and have such far-reaching repercussions, that leaders should give preference to them above all else. Whilst the importance of the symbolic frame is not doubted *for itself,* I take the view that structural, or indeed, human resource or political aspects, are *equivalently* important. Schein's broad view of organizational culture would seem to be out of kilter with the prevailing theory and research, outlined in Chapter 1, particularly with Sergiovanni's forces of leadership (p. 12) and his contention that *all* forces need to be present if leadership is to grow from competence to excellence. Schein's position also runs counter to the Bolman and Deal (1991) thesis which emphasizes that all four frames of reference are required to capture the full complexities of organizational leadership. Perhaps Schein and Johnson's views take a short-sighted, narrow approach which the Bolman and Deal model urges us to be wary of. It is the power to reframe, to take conscious account of all leadership perspectives which will be vital to success.

In contrast to Schein (1985) and Johnson (1990), I would argue that all four perspectives – structural, human resource, political, and symbolic – are interwoven in such a way that each separate dimension contributes to further enhance the other, with the collective result a complex, but amplified amalgamation. What this means is that *all four dimensions of leadership combine and intertwine to yield the full complexity of the leadership milieu. Any one dimension which is overlooked or disregarded will leave the picture incomplete, and leadership wanting.*

Following this reasoning, any form of leadership (autocratic, benevolent dictatorship, democratic) incorporates the four frames advocated by Bolman and Deal (1991). What distinguishes one leadership approach from another conceptually, and gives it its unique style and character, are the *specific elements* which are peculiar to it. Of particular interest in this discussion are the elements in each frame which form the basis of *collaborative* leadership.

The participating schools in this project, to a greater or lesser extent, were characterized by collaborative elements. Where a balance of all frames was present, fully-functioning collaborative leadership was operating. The findings indicate that at Kennedia Primary School, Clematis Secondary College and Boronia West High School strong collaborative leadership, across the school community, pervaded the day-to-day activities of the school.

Collaboration and School Success

In these schools, democratic processes and leadership density were actively cultivated by the principal and teacher, student and parent leaders. Roles and responsibilities were shared. Coordination and planning followed well-defined guidelines and policies, and programs were arrived at through clear, well communicated, shared processes. Frank, open and frequent communication prevailed, as did a respect and valuing for the opinions and viewpoints of others.

The centrality of teaching and learning was an integrating priority for leaders in these schools. To achieve the best for students, best practice was a continual goal. Cooperative teacher learning provided a base of mutual support and a springboard for professional challenge. Continuous learning and improvement were nurtured through support, acceptance, professional honesty and sharing. People worked in teams or workgroups, combining their expertise and experience to achieve their goals. Positive student/staff relationships, staff cohesion and a strong sense of community were apparent.

Leaders developed a school climate characterized by an absence of hierarchy. Participatory decision-making brought a sense of fairness to school processes, with accompanying opportunities to redress inequities and ensure alignment with the values and vision of the school. Power-sharing was actively promoted, through agreed-upon political behaviour. Coalitions and interest groups formed around issues, rather than individuals. Networks were established between cluster schools. Consensus was sought, diffusing conflict and the negative aspects of informal influence. There was an understanding that disagreements over issues were inevitable. Disputes were not seen as disruptive, but structures and processes needed to be firmly in place to ensure fair and just decisions. Authority was used to safeguard the beliefs and values of the school and to exert a positive influence.

Leaders held certain beliefs and values which guided the daily practice of these schools. An underpinning belief that disadvantaged children should have full educational opportunities, and that school arrangements could make this happen, was complemented by a deep-seated belief in the intrinsic value of each individual, student or staff member. There was a valuing of diversity and an acceptance of interdependence, an acceptance of the individual, and a high value placed on interpersonal openness. Attitudes of acceptance of differences, caring and respect, egalitarianism, inclusiveness and self-worth predominated. Norms of openness, interaction, socializing, cooperation and teamwork, mutual support, cohesion, professional pride and satisfaction in the job, and commitment and enthusiasm typified the way in which the administrators, teachers and students conducted themselves in their workplaces.

At Banksia Primary a collaborative culture was developing well, with many of the above elements institutionalized into the school culture. The leadership process of transforming the school culture to a collaborative one, needs time to take shape, and requires the commitment, not just of the principal, but across a breadth of leadership in the school.

Developing, maintaining and sustaining a collaborative culture takes time, and takes a good deal of effort from a good many people. Clematis Secondary, Kennedia Primary and Boronia West High Schools have achieved this. Banksia Primary School is in transition. At Cassinia Secondary College a collaborative culture had not been established. Whilst steps forward had been made in restoring the rift between the two staffs from the former technical and high schools, however, strong divisions were still evident. Although amongst some faculty groups a shared ideology existed, there was an absence of shared vision by all staff members. A perceived lack, by some members of staff, of articulation and communication of the vision of the school left people unsure of the direction in which the school was heading. '*We don't really know the philosophy of where the school wants to go – no school goals are written down*,' commented one teacher. Aspects of each of the frames were present, such as the centrality of teaching and learning, support for students, networking with cluster schools, however the absence of many other factors left the culture weak. It is worth reflecting as to why this might be so.

Judith Warren Little (1986:84ff) noted that schools where collaborative cultures exist are rare, and Firestone and Wilson (1985:7ff) point out that school cultures are typically weak. Johnson (1990:149ff) suggests a number of reasons for this. First, the double-sided responsibilities it entails, 'the short-term task of teaching students day-to-day and the long-term task of broadly educating them'. Johnson suggests the 'tension is considerable' between the two. The second reason comes from the organizational arrangements within the school such as 'withholding time, encouragement and responsibility'. Third, from teachers themselves who choose to operate in isolation from their colleagues and as Johnson explains,

> In broad terms the preferred culture of teaching is frequently not compatible with the prevailing context of teachers' work resulting in a situation where:
>
> successful and committed teachers have left the profession because their workplaces were inferior, confining, disheartening environments that prohibited them from doing the work they set out to do and that most people believe they should do (Johnson, 1990:xiv).

Richard Bates (1986) addresses the notion of the simultaneous presence of competing subcultures which can operate in schools. Fullan (1993) and Hargreaves (1994) alert us to co-existing cultures of isolation, balkanization and contrived collegiality. These writings could provide further insight into the nature of collaboration at Cassinia Secondary College, where a collaborative culture failed to establish.

Collaborative cultures in schools may generally be a rare occurrence, but at Clematis Secondary, Kennedia Primary and Boronia West High Schools collaborative cultures operated successfully. At this point, I would like to propose that the *reason* for success in establishing workplaces which provide professional stimulation and satisfaction, is due directly to the *collaborative leadership* which operates in those schools, and the development of an accompanying *fully functioning collaborative culture*. Moreover, as suggested in the synthesis of the hypothesized causal links in Chapter 8, these fully functioning collaborative cultures have put a priority on development of the educational potential of students which is directly linked to:

- *positive student behaviour;*
- *a climate conducive to learning;*
- *an innovative curriculum designed to meet student needs.*

professional development of teachers which directly linked to:

- *organizational fit;*
- *continuous teacher learning;*
- *professional satisfaction/love of teaching.*

good organizational health which is directly linked to:

- *a technical culture;*
- *harmonious relationships;*
- *effective management.*

institutionalization of vision which is directly linked to:

- *shared beliefs;*
- *leadership density;*
- *commitment, cooperation and support;*

all of which, in combination, generate success.

Clark and Meloy (1989:291ff) list the following 'musts' in imagining what they term 'the new school', that is one based on a democratic rather than a bureaucratic structure:

- A new school must be built on the assumption of the consent of the governed.
- A new school must be built on shared authority and responsibility, not on delegation of authority and responsibility.
- A staff of a new school must trade assignments and work in multiple groups to remain in touch with the school as a whole.
- Formal rewards to the staff – salary, tenure, forms of promotion – should be under the control of the staff of a new school as a whole.
- The goals of the new school must be formulated and agreed to through group consensus.

In Clark and Meloy's terms, student outcomes would be enhanced and school success would be achieved. School reform would be realized! But is this a realistic expectation? Can success be so easily won? The short answer would seem to be a clear 'no'. Further explanation is necessary. At the outset of this book a brief commentary on the evolution of leadership theory was traced from its beginnings as a task-focused exercise by a single, all-knowing leader, to the complex dimensions of cultural, symbolic, educational, human, technical leadership, broad-ranging, and operating in a transformational sense. The present knowledge base informs us that organizations, and schools in particular, are non-rational workplaces (Barth, 1990; Fullan, 1988; Holly and Southworth, 1989) where simple management recipes cannot be directly applied.

Success remains elusive without the additional key ingredient of *artistry*. To know when and how to apply the recipe requires artistry – an artistry which reads the idiosyncrasies of each leadership context, manipulates, manoeuvres and exploits the four frames according to need, brings checks and balances to the constantly changing, dynamic educational context, and pursues the initiatives which will see the vision realized. Through single frames, or with rational application alone, only partial success can be achieved in accomplishing a fully functioning collaborative culture. Leaders need to know when one dimension should take precedence over another; what emphases are needed and for how long; leaders need to manage the integration of the leadership milieu – how structure relates to human factors, which relate to politics, which impinge on the symbolic, and so forth, and the multiple computations and permutations which are produced. Further, leaders need to do more than just *know about* all this, they need to have the ability and skill to *do* it, to put it into action, and to do it every day; day in, day out. As Bolman and Deal (1991:450) state 'success requires artistry, skill, and the ability to see organizations as organic forms in which needs, roles, power and symbols must be combined to provide direction and shape behaviour.' Holly and Southworth (1989:64) confirm this position. 'If the head is orchestrator of all the other leaders and members then maybe the school will work in greater harmony.' Starratt captures the character of the artistry required for leadership in the urban schools participating in this project:

> the leader sees his or her primary task as influencing the way people in the institution see themselves and see what they have to do. This means raising questions, challenging assumptions, asking for another opinion, looking beyond tomorrow's solution to the larger challenge. The leader must become something of a Socratic gadfly, bothering people enough until they begin to think things through more thoroughly, discuss them together, take the time to appreciate the significance of what they are doing. The new leader must orchestrate a more intense and thorough-going group think (1993:148).

On the basis of the outcomes of the related theory and research presented throughout this book, as well as my own professional experience in leadership roles in schools, discerning application of Bolman and Deal's model of leadership is recommended to assist those already in and those aspiring to leadership positions. Bolman and Deal's structural, human resource, political and symbolic dimensions provide a practical framework for interpretation of personal practice and a valuable means of identifying areas for professional development. In the first instance the framework would aid leaders in making sense of the world in which they work, a complex one at the best of times, and a bewildering and stressful one in the present tumultuous circumstances facing schools. Guidance can be gained from looking at this seemingly uninterpretable world from structural, human resource, political and symbolic viewpoints, bringing a focus where there does not appear to be one. Second, implementation and perceptive use of the Bolman and Deal frames can provide opportunities at the personal level for leaders to reflect upon and interpret their own preferred leadership behaviour, reframing to avoid any blind-spots, enlarging both their insight and their repertoire of skills, and thereby increasing their professional effectiveness.

It is acknowledged that leadership is a difficult and complex business. Hargreaves (1995:1) offers an interpretation of leadership through the notion of *paradox* where he sees our present educational environment as one full of paradoxes 'symptomatic of a world in rapid transformation – pulling us in many directions at the same time'. Hargreaves (1995) quotes an insightful Charles Handy who eloquently asserts:

> The acceptance of paradox as a feature of our life is the first step towards living with it and managing it . . . We can and should reduce the starkness of some of the contradictions, minimize the inconsistencies, understand the puzzles in the paradoxes, but we cannot make them disappear, nor solve them completely, nor escape from them . . . Paradoxes are like the weather, something to be lived with, not solved, the worst aspects mitigated, the best enjoyed and used as clues to the way forward. Paradox has to be *accepted*, coped with and made sense of, in life, in work, in community and among nations (1994:17–18).

Given the complexities of effective leadership in the global context in which education resides, a framework to bring reason and insight to the leadership milieu is pressing. What is being proposed in this book is, that *given this context – and because of it*, reframing and artistry go some of the way to make sense of the complexities and bring a degree of rationality to it. In combining artistry with the use of the Bolman and Deal frames, school leaders should go a long way to see this happen. At this point I would like to offer some thoughts for reflection.

Issues for Reflection

The above is a summarized commentary delineating the positive, and what I consider to be the critical features of successful leadership in schools of the 1990s. It is an account of effective leadership behaviour in a fast-moving organizational world of change and uncertainty, and it goes a good deal of the way to rationalize an otherwise paradoxical context. That in itself is a big step forward, not to be underestimated. Continuing reflection, however, would seem to be mandatory as more and more of the leadership picture is unveiled, and as our world descends on and bombards us with challenges never seen before.

Collaboration and Empowerment

It would seem crucial to address some issues related to empowerment. The contention promoted in this book is one of a leadership structure encompassing widespread empowerment. This has enormous ramifications for the practice of leadership. Making it work is a complex undertaking, for it means making a shift from the traditional top-down line of hierarchical leadership and management to a more open and diverse structure. Power and authority are shared, and lie in the hands of many, and the school is 'characterized by an integrated approach to organizational structure where ideas from multiple sources are combined into meaningful wholes' (Wallace and Wildy, 1995:15). Patterns of leadership are collaborative and focus on facilitating the shared purposes of the school. Group tasks and responsibilities are directed toward innovation and experimentation, *improvement* (not maintenance) being a foremost expectation, centred around teams and workgroups which are formed and disbanded according to need. Expertise and interest, rather than seniority or formal status, dictate the membership of each team or workgroup. For many, this shift is a threatening and perplexing one. Most of us work in situations where there is a top-down structure with a matching line of accountability. Moving to a democratically organized organization at first sight appears to deny the benefits that line management can bring to governance. To those who have not witnessed the alternative, disbanding traditional bureaucratic structures seems a rash and reckless move. The evidence, however, stands overwhelmingly in favour of taking steps towards doing just that, and we ignore the evidence at our peril. If the research consistently points out to us that *effective schools are effective because of their capacity to build a collaborative culture*, can we deny that this applies to *our* school? Can we disregard the best practice in schools elsewhere because it does not appeal to us and may be a little discomforting? When the facts to the contrary are staring us in the face, then answer must be a clear and emphatic 'No!', uncomfortable though it may be. So, if we are true to our ourselves as professionals, we must accommodate a re-thinking of our position, and this must be accompanied by a reorganization of structures; structures which are arranged to support attitudes of broad-ranging inclusiveness, bringing dispersed empowerment and responsibility to staff, parents, and students alike. Strongly focused leadership is imperative to make this happen. The role of the leader becomes more one of a group facilitator, communicator, team-builder, problem-solver, information sharer, ideas promoter, encourager, energy sustainer, conflict resolver and resource finder, who can gain the participation and commitment of others to the shared purposes. This, of course, will not be a single-handed leadership. It will be collective leadership where the combined strengths of the leadership team are pooled to achieve the task at hand.

Collaboration and the Classroom

One area that has not been pursued in this book is the natural extension of the concept of collaboration to the culture of the classroom, in particular with regard to the relationship between teacher and students. It has crossed my mind that as the *adult* culture of the school (school council, principal, teachers and administration) becomes collaborative, school reform may remain impotent if the relationship between adults and children does not, in turn, embrace the same principles and develop collaborative relationships, not just in terms of student participation in decision-making, but in terms of organizing student learning in the classroom. By this I mean that if an autocratic, teacher-directed learning culture exists in a school, even though there is a collaborative administrative culture, we are falling short of the mark. The central focus of school improvement is, and must be, student learning. It has been already shown in this book that there are quite direct, positive outcomes for students which flow from a collaborative adult culture, and these are significant. However, it would seem to me that a good next step might be to investigate the nature of a collaborative *student* culture in the classroom. Experience has indicated that we can be more effective as teachers if we shift our mindset from what is often seen as teacher territory to what could be legitimately called student territory, namely, the learning spaces and, indeed, the curriculum of the classroom and school environs.

I think principles of collaboration should apply at all levels, with special significance for the adolescent and senior levels. If you have taught at these levels then you will know that it is quite possible to maintain class control and dispense portions of knowledge to students; knowledge which they digest and then regurgitate so that it can be assessed accordingly. Students of this age and stage have learnt the ground rules of what is expected of them in terms of classroom behaviour and what it is that they need to 'learn'. They well understand the sanctions that will be imposed if those expectations are breached, so they conform. On the surface all goes along according to plan, but I would like to suggest that in many instances we do our students an injustice with this approach and deny them any real engagement in learning which is relevant and meaningful to them as individuals. The introduction of technology, particularly computer technology, magnifies this position. It is somewhat dismaying for teachers to find that, with home computers, some students have access to vast data bases of knowledge, and can learn more at home than they do at school; that the parameters of their learning are broadened far beyond the classroom and far beyond the formal control and constraints inherent in lock-step, linear school-based curriculum directed by teachers.

Another observation I have made is that student sub-cultures have enormous informal power, dramatically influencing the formal teacher-directed culture. If active student participation and self-directed learning is denied to students through traditional teaching methodologies, then invariably they will go underground to compensate for this deficiency; a deficiency which denies them their uniqueness as individuals, and their diversity as a group. Going underground may take the form of discipline problems either inside or outside the classroom, or, it may mean that a sub-culture emerges with a 'them and us' mentality, students versus staff. It also means that the student norm of '*school learning is not cool*' takes hold and that lip service only is paid to classroom learning; any chance of 'learning how to learn' and becoming lifelong learners, despite the best efforts of teachers, becomes slim. Teachers as a professional group, particularly at the secondary level, have been slow to adopt collaborative teaching practices, so perhaps not surprisingly, it is not educationalists but *technological* forces outside the school (such as home computers with, for example, access to multi-media, electronic mail and Internet), which are shaping the classroom of the future. Teachers may be either exhilarated or threatened by this. Whichever it is, change will not only come, it has actually arrived, and if teachers really are to serve the students of today and the future, serious and committed attention must be given to the way in which their role as a teacher shifts from one of 'font and controller of all knowledge', to one of facilitator, mentor, resourcer, learner and sharer of knowledge. That is, promoting collaborative patterns of teaching and learning in their classrooms.

Collaboration – Why is it so Rare?

Knowing About it is One Thing, and Doing it Yourself is Another

As a school leader myself, I have thought carefully about the issues woven between the pages of this book, and whilst my own professional experience has not been based in inner-city schools, most of what is said rings remarkably true to my own practice. To a large extent I believe the understandings presented in this book to be universal, and, as such, are of significance to us all. As a school leader, I am deeply committed to trying to practice what I preach in my own school setting. I have found the process of reculturing to collaborative patterns of leadership as beguiling and elusive as the research continually indicates. A major need is to transfer your thinking from highly legitimate and inspiring theoretical insights to a practical mindset of knowing *what collaboration is, and how to **do** it at an operational level*. It is as if you have to institutionalize the body of leadership theory in your own mind into a *personal* theory of leadership so that you can carry it around with you in your head at all times, to make sense of what is happening around you on a day-to-day, hour-by-hour, and sometimes minute-by-minute basis! I have found the Bolman and Deal framework of inordinate value in this respect. As well, taking time for reflection to clearly identify specific collaborative elements within this framework has enabled me to see the reality of *the extent of the job to be done* in developing and sustaining a collaborative culture. I have seen collaboration limited to consultation and a few more staff appointments at the senior level. Not surprisingly it has been found to be ineffective, and sadly, rejected. Collaboration itself is not to blame, but a inadequate interpretation of what it entails. I am anxious to see that collaboration is not reduced to superficialities, with accompanying oversimplification and underestimation of the task and inevitable failure. As a result, this book has been dedicated to unravelling the complexities involved and intends only to give a preliminary glimpse of the operational dimensions of what constitutes collaborative leadership. Further insights will unfold as others take up the issues and proffer their points of view.

Change

Reculturing the school means moving from one environment through a process of change to another. Whether you move out of an isolationist, balkanized, innovative, autocratic or other type of organizational culture to a collaborative one, it is *by necessity* accompanied by change – change coexists; change cohabits. Like love and (successful) marriage – you can't have one without the other. There is a coexistence between *reculturing* and change. In addition, change is not only fundamental to the *establishment* of a collaborative culture, but by its very nature, change is *integral to the processes of* collaboration itself, and to the sustaining of the culture. Collaborative leadership sets out to improve rather than maintain what is happening in schools, therefore, management of change is an essential element. So, it is critical that the basic lessons learnt in regard to leading and managing the change process (for example, Fullan, 1993; Miles, 1987) are heeded. This is a pre-condition to success. *Understandings associated with the management of change form a critical connection to the successful implementation of a collaborative culture.* It is simply not possible to mandate a belief or a commitment whether it be to collaboration or anything else. Change is developmental and takes place over time and is implemented by individual people who will only take it on board at their own pace. (Some will never do so). Given this position, working towards a fully functioning collaborative culture is a slow, sometimes halting process, and depends upon the pre-existing culture of the school and the people within it, as to how many years it may take to achieve. Patience and persistence play an important part. Moving into collaborative cultures without due respect being given to the processes of change is destined to fail.

Vision

When the collaborative stage is set, the curtain rises with the instigation of a *shared vision.* Terms such as 'vision' and 'mission' are endlessly bandied about and sometimes confusing. Whatever you call it, there has to be some sustained deep moral purpose guiding the beliefs, values and attitudes and norms of behaviour in a school. This must be the driving force for its very existence, and the central focus of people's energy and commitment. In my view, once decided, this moral purpose is *non-negotiable* in the medium to long term. In the inner city schools of this study, the vision was crystal clear – *a belief that disadvantaged children should have full educational opportunities and that school arrangements can make this happen.* Non-negotiable. Unwavering. Unmoved by postmodern paradoxes, uncertainties or 'terrifying times'. It is a given. I don't believe that this deeply held belief will be superseded nor become redundant in the near or even distant future. How to translate it into practice? How to implement it? Well that's an entirely different story. Here I support Hargreaves's (1995:4) proposition of 'moving missions' where 'teachers and schools should review and renew their purposes over time, along with the social contexts in which these purposes are embedded.' I would make a clear distinction, however, between the higher order purpose *that disadvantaged children should have full educational opportunities and that school arrangements can make this happen*, and that of what I would call comparatively lower order purpose, such as *using school structures to address and support children's learning*. Lower order purposes are operational rather than social or moral and are, therefore, negotiable – open for discussion and appropriate to change at any point of time – and, importantly, to ensure effective implementation. Both are shared visions, the latter evolving, the former something of a universal truth. In short, I embrace Drucker's (1993:53) some-times unpopular view that 'the organization must be single-minded, otherwise its members become confused . . . only a clear focused and common mission can hold the organization together and enable it to produce results'. I would argue that this is a legitimate position to hold, and that it can, not only take an appropriate place in schools of the postmodern age, but actively lead to their success. However, strictly held beliefs must be accompanied by the flexibility of 'moving missions' so that current contexts and conditions can accommodate their institutionalization into the daily practices of the school. Artistry once again is called for to see that the same tightness which relates to vision should not pervade the general operations of the school. In terms of translating the vision into the day-to-day activities of the school, flexibility, creativity, problem-solving and artistry come into play. 'Moving missions' *are* needed, as Hargreaves has pointed out, to face an educational world in which we constantly encounter hair-raising challenges, and which we are obliged to confront in order to achieve success. A leader's capacity to hold fast to the moral, social or spiritual vision of the school, and at the same time be flexible, creative and problem-solve at the operational level contributes directly to school success.

I would venture to add that misunderstandings of the relationship be-tween tight and loose functions of collaborative leadership lead to collabora-tion's sometimes poor image in some circles of practice, which insist that it simply doesn't work. In fact, it is a naivety of approach that brings the down-fall of so-called collaborative efforts. Being collaborative means being single-minded and passionate – single-minded about the school's moral purpose and passionate in the vigilance, determination and resolve which is required to see the vision executed. What is needed for leadership here is well described by Martin Luther King as 'a tough mind and a tender heart'.

Empowerment

The reconceptualization of the concept of leadership to include the notion of 'leadership density' has far-reaching effects for leaders in schools. It means a re-thinking of attitudes to accommodate a redistribution of power. Structures can be implemented to support attitudes of broad-ranging inclusiveness, bringing distributed empowerment and responsibility to staff, parents, and students.

Changes to attitudes, however, are not easily achieved as history shows. Nonetheless, it is worth emphasizing that the findings of this book indicate that where the school culture is immersed in a belief in the democratic process, a valuing of the individual, a valuing of diversity, and where interpersonal openness and caring and respect are the norm, school success, even under the most trying conditions, can be won. It would seem there is inherent wisdom for school leaders to attend to the pervasive attitudes which permeate their schools. However, the doing of it is difficult, as it really challenges *all* within the organization to deliberately take a stand on what they believe leadership *is*. It is not sufficient for theorists or researchers to know that empowerment is integral to achieving success in a school, everyone else in the school workplace has to believe it too. Effort must be made to ensure that empowerment as a concept is sanctioned and becomes embedded in the values base of those making decisions in the school. There needs to be a shared understanding and acceptance by teachers, students and parents, as well as the formal leadership team, that dispersed power sharing is, in fact, an effective and rightful thing to do if you want to gainfully bring about improvement in your school. Like our reluctance to give up control in the classroom, moving away from the hierarchical way we have worked for generations is such a radical change that it is disorienting and discomforting. Nonetheless, examples of best practice persistently point to the fact that empowerment at the school and classroom level is essential if actual growth and development is to take place. We cannot put our heads in the sand and pretend that it does not apply to us. Until there is a *state of readiness*, however, to take on the responsibility associated with empowerment, fully functioning collaboration must wait in the wings. This responsibility demands acceptance of, and commitment to, the basic features of collaboration, such as taking a whole school focus, working with others in a democratic way to achieve a shared vision, valuing and respecting others' opinions, frequent communication and sharing of information, working towards consensus and so on. Once again, caution is necessary at the outset. It is not a matter of whole-scale handing over of power to anyone who wants it. Accompanying responsibilities and accountability run alongside any sharing of power, otherwise direction will become fragmented, informal power groups will take hold, and chaos reign.

Given the above, it is necessary to reflect on what happens to the hierarchy when widespread sharing of power is in place. Fullan (1993) suggests a *top-down, bottom-up approach* where a composite of both centralization and decentralization forces operate. He proposes that neither centralization or decentralization work. This applies internally within the school (curriculum development; strategic planning) and to external forces operating outside the school (government policy changes and directives). Fullan's proposition has a lot to offer the practice as, apart from expecting to deal with imposition, it can help to provide a balanced perspective which leaders, immersed and isolated in the immediate demands of their frenetic workplaces, might otherwise overlook.

Fullan (1993) also highlights another point which is of significance to the whole notion of collaboration, namely that 'individualism and collectivism must have equal power'. This is worth commenting on as it links directly with two values expressed as fundamental to collaboration in the symbolic frame of this book – valuing the uniqueness of each individual, and valuing diversity. Fullan makes the point that leaders need to work with 'polar opposites', that there are no 'one-sided solutions'. Again it is a matter of balance. Leaders who assume collaboration will always be a collective activity will see only part of the picture. The creative, original and inner thought that comes from the individual mind should not be overpowered by the group. Groupthink has the potential to be dangerous and needs to be moderated by individual reasoning. As Fullan points out, groups are powerful, but they may be powerfully wrong. It is often said that leaders should take note of the devil's advocate on their staff. Listening and taking account of the non-conforming view brings a perspective to light that may be swept away by mainstream thought.

Collaboration and Social and Moral Belief

One last reflection that requires considered attention relates to Nias *et al*'s (1989:73) statement that collaborative attitudes 'arise from and embody a set of social and moral beliefs about desirable relationships between individuals and the community of which they are a part, not from beliefs about epistemology and pedagogy.' In other words, Nias and her colleagues have insightfully discerned that critical factors to successful collaborative leadership have their roots in the contributing disciplines of leadership theory – sociology, social psychology, political science and social and cultural anthropology, *not in theories of learning and teaching*. This notion would seem to me to be of dramatic significance. Maybe we are looking in the wrong place for our exemplar leaders. Maybe *before* their need to be *au fait* with sound technical practice, sophisticated organizational and political skills, leaders need to be aware of who they are themselves *as people first* – what values they hold dear, what motivates them in their life's choices and priorities, and how they will respond to given sets of circumstances. If, for argument's sake, valuing of individuality, diversity, participation, community, trust and risk taking are not *personally* held beliefs by leaders in their schools, it is difficult to imagine how those leaders could establish or sustain a collaborative culture in their school. Norms of interaction, cooperation, mutual support, staff–student–parent cohesion, interpersonal openness, commitment and enthusiasm are unlikely to develop unless leaders in schools model and actively promote those norms themselves. Equally, attitudes of acceptance, caring and respect, egalitarianism, inclusiveness, self-worth will probably not become institutionalized if there is not a pervading belief that these things are beneficial.

It is somewhat discomforting as a professional to contemplate the view that epistemology and pedagogy might play a less dominant role in effecting a collaborative culture than leaders' broader personally held beliefs about what is desirable as a society. Epistemology and pedagogy are, after all, at the heart of our work in schools. They are the bread and butter of our professional world, the focus of our attention, and one would expect that they would form the parameters of our professional thought. However, the influence and impact of a leader's moral and social beliefs cannot be overlooked. It gives serious food for thought.

The issues raised in the last part of this chapter reflect some of the reasons why a fully functioning culture is a rare occurrence. We are just beginning to address the realities of collaborative leadership in its day-to-day operational form. The time ahead offers enormous opportunity for school leaders to take up the attendant issues which present themselves. In doing so a pattern of leadership will be established which promotes cooperative sharing, communicating, problem-solving, management of change, continuous curriculum development and professional learning. *Collegial school-based working groups, with joint purposes, positively influence the quality of learning offered to the students in their schools*, and, as a result, the educational agenda is significantly advanced for students, for teachers and for the school as an organization.

In Conclusion

This book has set out to travel a not so well-trodden path. Much has been written about leadership; much has been written about culture; and much has been written about school effectiveness and success. The contribution of this book has been to identify a particular conception of leadership, namely *collaborative leadership*, and to establish in detail exactly what it is that collaborative leaders do in their schools, seemingly against all the odds, to generate success for their students, staff and organization. In addition, I have extended these findings into hypothesized causal links, which when synthesized, offer four distinctive factors as fundamental to a *fully functioning collaborative culture*, namely, development of educational potential, professional development of teachers, good organizational health and institutionalization of vision.

Collaborative leadership in this book is interpreted through four central forces of leadership – structural, human resource, political and symbolic. For collaborative leadership each force is critical to the whole, and each is expanded by its relationship with the other; the whole being not simply a sum of the parts. Moreover, the elements of the four frames of leadership, denote its collaborative character and style. The findings from the five project schools clearly indicate that quite specific leader behaviour can lead to success in schools. However, if full success is to be achieved, artistry is required to know when and how to exercise the various components of leadership so that a collaborative culture which brings success can be developed, sustained and maintained in the school. Sarros (1993:52) sums it up:

Leadership is a beguiling, perplexing, and challenging phenomenon. Exercised with discretion and consideration, leadership is a powerful tool in building a confident and committed workforce and a strong and resilient organisational culture. Leaders have immense impact on social and cultural systems, and therefore they're morally bound to exercise leadership with discretion and consideration of the general good, not the individual triumph.

In simpler terms, Robert Fulgham's credo taken from *All I Really Need to Know I Learned In Kindergarten* (1990) is of great appeal:

When you go out into the world, watch out for traffic, hold hands and stick together.

References

ARGYRIS, C. (1984) *Integrating the Individual and the Organisation*, New York: Wiley.

AUSTRALIAN PRINCIPALS ASSOCIATION PROFESSIONAL DEVELOPMENT COUNCIL (1993) *Leaders and their Learning: Professional Development Priorities for Principals*, Somerten Park: South Australia, Glenelg Press, (edited by Evans, B.).

BALL, S. (1987) *The Micro Politics of the School*, London: Methuen.

BANKSIA PRIMARY SCHOOL (1990) *School Council Annual Report.*

BARNARD, C.I. (1938) *The Functions of the Executive*, Cambridge, MA: Harvard University Press.

BARTH, R. (1990) *Improving Schools From Within*, San Francisco, CA: Jossey-Bass.

BATES, R.J. (1986) *The Management of Culture and Knowledge*, Waurn Ponds, Victoria: Deakin University Press.

BATES, R. (1993) 'Educational Administration as Cultural Practice', Australian College of Education: ACT, Australia, Occasional Paper No. 20.

BEARE, H., CALDWELL, B.J. and MILLIKAN, R.H. (1989) *Creating an Excellent School*, London: Routledge.

BENNIS, W. and NANUS, B. (1985) *Leaders: Strategies for Taking Charge*, New York: Harper and Row.

BOLMAN, L.G. and DEAL, T.E. (1991) *Reframing Organizations: Artistry, Choice and Leadership*, San Francisco, CA: Jossey-Bass.

BURNS, J.M. (1978) *Leadership*, New York: Harper & Row.

CALDWELL, B.J. and SPINKS, J.M. (1988) *The Self-Managing School*, London: Falmer Press.

CALDWELL, B.J. and SPINKS, J.M. (1992) *Leading The Self-Managing School*, London: Falmer Press.

CHENG, Y.C. (1993) 'Principal's leadership as a critical factor for school performance: Evidence from multi-levels of primary schools', Paper presented at the International Congress for School Effectiveness and Improvement, Norrkoping, Sweden, January.

CLARK, C. and YINGER, R. (1977) 'Research on teacher thinking', *Curriculum Inquiry*, 7, 4, pp. 279–304.

CLARK, D.L. and MELOY, J.M. (1989) 'Renouncing bureaucracy: A democratic structure for leadership in schools', in SERGIOVANNI, T.J. and MOORE, J.H. (Eds) *Schooling for Tomorrow: Directing Reforms to Issues that Count*, Boston, MA: Allen and Bacon.

COOPER, M. (1989) 'Whose culture is it, anyway?', in LIEBERMAN, A. (Ed) *Building a Professional Culture In Schools*, New York: Teachers College Press.

CROWTHER, F. and GIBSON, I. (1990) 'Research as problem discovery: discovering self-as-author through naturalistic inquiry', in MACPHERSON, R.J.S. and WEEKS, J. (Eds) *Pathways To Knowledge In Educational Administration: Methodologies and Research in Progress in Australia*, Melbourne: Australian Council for Educational Administration.

DEAL, T.E. (1990) 'Healing the schools: Restoring the heart', in LIEBERMAN, A. (Ed) *Schools as Collaborative Cultures: Creating the Future Now*, London: Falmer Press.

DEAL, T. and KENNEDY, A. (1982) *Corporate Cultures*, New York: Addison-Wesley.

DEAL, T.E. and PETERSON, K.D. (1990) *The Principal's Role in Shaping School Culture*, Washington, DC: United States Department of Education.

DEBNEY PARK HIGH SCHOOL (1986) *Human Rights*, Victoria: PEP Schools Resource Program. DEPARTMENT OF EDUCATION OF VICTORIA (1985) Ministerial Papers. Victoria: Ministry of Education.

DEVELOPMENT COUNCIL (1993) Leaders and their Learning: Professional Development Priorities for Principals, Somerten Park: South Australia, Glenelg Press.

DRUCKER, P. (1993) *Post – Capitalist Society*, New York: Teachers' College Press.

FIEDLER, F.E. (1967) *A Theory Of Leadership Effectiveness*, New York: McGraw-Hill.

FIRESTONE, W.A. and WILSON, B.L. (1985) 'Using bureaucratic linkages to improve instruction: The principal's contribution', *Educational Administration Quarterly*, **21**, 2, pp. 7–13.

FOLLETT, M.P. (1941) *Dynamic Administration: The Collected Papers of Mary Parker Follett*, METCALF, H. and URLWICK, L. (Eds) New York: Harper and Row.

FULGHUM, R. (1990) *All I Really Need to Know I Learned In Kindergarten*, New York: Villard Books.

FULLAN, M.G. (1988) *What's Worth Fighting For In The Principalship?: Strategies For Taking Charge In The Elementary School Principalship*, Toronto: Ontario Public School Teachers' Federation.

FULLAN, M.G. (1991) *The New Meaning of Educational Change*, London: Cassell.

FULLAN, M.G. (1993) *Change Forces: Probing the Depths of Educational Reform*, London: Falmer Press.

FULLAN, M.G. and HARGREAVES, A. (Eds) (1991a) *Understanding Teacher Development*, London: Cassell.

FULLAN, M.G. and HARGREAVES, A. (1991b) *What's Worth Fighting For?: Working Together For Your School*, Toronto: Ontario Public School Teachers' Federation.

FULLAN, M.G. and HARGREAVES, A. (Eds) (1992) *Teacher Development and Educational Change*, London: Falmer Press.

FULLAN, M.G., BENNETT, B. and ROLHEISER-BENNETT, C. (1990) 'Linking classroom and school improvement', *Educational Leadership*, **47**, 8, pp. 13–19.

GIDDENS, A. (1979) *Central Problems in Social Theory: Action, Structure and Contradictions in Social Analysis*, London: Macmillan.

GOFFMAN, E. (1974) *Frame Analysis*, Cambridge, MA: Harvard University Press.

GOODLAD, J.I. (1984) *A Place Called School: Prospects for the Future*, New York: McGraw-Hill.

GREENFIELD, T.B. (1986) 'Leaders and schools: Willfullness and non-natural order in organizations', in SERGIOVANNI, T.J. and CORBALLY, J.E. (Eds) *Leadership and Organizational Cultures: New Perspectives on Administrative Theory and Practice*, Chicago, IL: University of Chicago Press.

GRONN, P. (1995) 'Greatness re-visited: The current obsession with transformational leadership', in *Leading and Managing, Journal of the Australian Council for Educational Administration*, **1**, 1, Autumn.

HANDY, C. (1985) *Understanding Organisations*, London: Penguin.

HANDY, C. (1994) *The Empty Raincoat*, London: Hutchison.

HARGREAVES, A. (1994) *Changing Teachers, Changing Times: Teacher's Work and Culture in the Postmodern Age*, Cassell: London.

HARGREAVES, A. (1995) *Changing Teachers, Changing Times: Strategies for Leadership in an Age of Paradox, ACEA Seminar Notes*, Melbourne: June.

HARGREAVES, A. and DAWE, R. (1990) 'Paths of professional development: Contrived collegiality collaborative culture, and the case of peer coaching', *Teaching and Teacher Education*, **6**, 3, pp. 20–34.

HERSEY, P. and BLANCHARD, K. (1982) *Management of Organizational Behaviour: Utilizing Human Resources*, (4th Edition) Englewood Cliffs, NJ: Prentice Hall.

HOCKING, H. and CALDWELL, B.J. (1990) 'Conceptual frameworks', in MACPHERSON, R.J.S. and WEEKS, J. (Eds) *Pathways To Knowledge In Educational Administration: Methodologies and Research in Progress in Australia*, Armidale, New South Wales: ACEA.

HOLLY, P. and SOUTHWORTH, G. (1989) *The Developing School*, London: Falmer Press.

HOUSE, E. and LAPAN, S. (1978) *Survival in the Classroom*, Boston, MA: Allen and Unwin.

HOYLE, E. (1986) *The Politics of School Management*, Milton Keynes: Open University.

HUBERMAN, M. (1983) 'Recipes for busy kitchens', *Knowledge: Creation, Diffusion, Utilization*, **4**, pp. 478–510.

HUBERMAN, M. (1991) 'Teacher development and instructional mastery', in HARGREAVES, A. and FULLAN, M., *Understanding Teacher Development*, London: Cassell.

JOHNSON, S.M. (1990) *Teachers' Work: Achieving Success in Our Schools*, New York: Basic Books.

KANTER, R.M. (1977) *Men and Women of the Corporation*, New York: Basic Books.

KOTTER, J.P. (1990) *A Force For Change: How Leadership Differs from Management*, London and New York: The Free Press.

LEITHWOOD, K. (1992) 'The principal's role in teacher development', in FULLAN, M. and HARGREAVES, A. (Eds) (1992) *Teacher Development and Educational Change*, London: Falmer Press.

LEITHWOOD, K. (1994) 'Leadership for school restructuring', Paper presented at the International Congress for School Effectiveness and Improvement, Melbourne, Australia, January.

LEITHWOOD, K. and JANTZI, D. (1990) 'Transformational leadership: How principals can reform school culture', Paper presented at the Annual Meeting of the American Educational Research Association Annual Meeting.

LEITHWOOD, K. BEGLEY, P.T. and COUSINS, J.B. (1992) *Developing Expert Leadership for Future Schools*, London: Falmer Press.

LITTLE, J. (1982) 'Norms of collegiality and experimentation: Workplace conditions of school success', *American Educational Research Journal*, **19**, pp. 235–40.

LITTLE, J. (1986) 'Seductive images and organizational realities in professional development', *Teachers College Record*, **86**, 1, pp. 84–102.

LITTLE, J. (1990) 'The persistence of privacy: Autonomy and initiative in teachers' professional relations', *Teachers College Record*, **91**, 4, pp. 509–36.

LORTIE, D. (1975) *School Teacher: A Sociological Book*, Chicago, IL: University of Chicago Press.

LOUIS, K. and MILES, M.B. (1991) 'Managing reform: Lessons from urban high schools', *School Effectiveness and Improvement*, **2**, 1, pp. 75–96.

MCGEGOR, D. (1960) *The Human Side of Enterprise*, New York: McGraw-Hill.

MARSHALL, G. and ROSSMAN, G. (1989) *Designing Qualitative Research*, Newbury Park, CA: Sage.

MIDDLETON, M. (1982) *Marking Time*, Melbourne: Methuen Australia.

MILES, M.B. (1987) 'Practical guidelines for school administrators: How to get there', Paper read at a symposium of Effective Schools Programs and the Urban High School. Washington, DC: Annual Meeting of the American Research Association.

MILES, M.B. and HUBERMAN, A.M. (1984) *Qualitative Data Analysis: A Sourcebook of New Methods*, Beverly Hills, CA: Sage.

MINISTRY OF EDUCATION (1985) 'Ministerial Paper Number 4:4.5', Publishing Services, Statewide School Support and Production Centre, Victoria, Australia.

MINTZBERG, H. (1973) *The Nature of Managerial Work*, New York: Harper and Row.

MORRIS, L.L., FITZ-GIBBON, C. and FREEMAN, M. (1987) *How to Communicate Evaluation Findings*, Newbury Park, CA: Sage.

NIAS, J., SOUTHWORTH, G. and YEOMANS, R. (1989) *Staff Relationships in the Primary Schools*, London: Cassell.

OWENS, R.G. (1991) *Organizational Behaviour in Education*, (4th Edition) Englewood Cliffs, NJ: Prentice-Hall.

PETERS, T.J. and WATERMAN, R.H., JR (1982) *In Search of Excellence: Lessons from America's Best-Run Companies*, New York: Harper and Row.

PURKEY, S.C. and SMITH, M.S. (1985) 'School reform: The district policy implications of the effective schools literature', *The Elementary School Journal*, **85**, 3, pp. 353–89.

ROBBINS, S.P. (1989) *Organizational Behaviour*, London: Prentice-Hall.

ROSENHOLTZ, S. (1989) *Teachers' Workplace: The Social Organization Of Schools*, New York: Longman.

SANDERSON HIGH SCHOOL (1988) *Sanderson High School: A Case Book In Effective Schooling*, Darwin: Northern Territory Department of Education.

SARROS, J.C. (1993) 'Essential characteristics of successful leaders', *The Educational Administrator*, **38**, pp. 36–52.

SCHEIN, E.H. (1985) *Organizational Culture and Leadership: A Dynamic View*, San Francisco, CA: Jossey-Bass.

SCHOOLS COUNCIL (1990) 'Australia's teachers: An agenda for the next decade', A Paper prepared by the Schools Council for the National Board of Employment, Education and Training, Canberra: Australian Government Publishing Service.

SERGIOVANNI, T.J. (1984) 'Leadership and Excellence in Schooling', *Educational Leadership*, **41**, 5, pp. 4–13.

SERGIOVANNI, T.J. (1987) 'The theoretical basis for cultural leadership', in SHEIVE, L.T. and SCHOENHEIT, M.B. (Eds) *1987 Yearbook of the Association for Supervision and Curriculum Development*, Alexandria, VA: ASCA.

SERGIOVANNI, T.J. (1990) *Value-Added Leadership: How to Get Extraordinary Results in Schools*, New York: Harcourt Brace Jovanovich.

SERGIOVANNI, T.J. and STARRATT, R.J. (1988) *Supervision: Human Perspectives*, (*4th* Edition) New York: McGraw-Hill.

STAKE, R.E. (1967) 'The countenance of educational evaluation', in SHADISH, W.R., JR, COOK, T.D. and LEVITON, L.C. (1991) *Foundations of Program Evaluation Theories of Practice*, Newbury Park, CA: Sage.

STARRATT, R.J. (1991) 'Building an ethical school: A theory for practice in educational leadership', *Educational Administration Quarterly*, **27**, 2, pp. 185–202.

STARRATT, R.J. (1993) *The Drama of Leadership*, London: Falmer Press.

STOGDILL, R.M. (1974) *Handbook of Leadership: A Survey of the Literature*, New York: Free Press.

TAYLOR, F. (1911) *The Principles of Scientific Management*, New York: Harper and Row.

WALLACE, J. and WILDY, H. (1995) 'The changing world of leadership: Working in a professional organisation today', in *The Practising Administrator: Journal of the Australian Council for Educational Administration*, **17**, 1.

WATKINS, P. (1985) *Agency and Structure: Dialectics in the Administration of Education*, Geelong, Victoria: Deakin University Press.

WATKINS, P. (1989) 'Leadership, power and symbols in educational administration', in SMYTH, J. (Ed) (1989) *Critical Perspectives on Educational Leadership*, London: Falmer Press.

WIDEEN, M.F. (1992) 'School-based teacher development', in FULLAN, M.G. and HARGREAVES, A. (Eds) (1992) *Teacher Development and Educational Change*, London: Falmer Press.

YUKL, G. (1989) 'Managerial leadership: A review of theory and research', *Journal of Management*, **15**, 2, pp. 251–89.

Appendixes

Appendix 1:   School Profile

Profile of your School

The Task

In this document we ask you to provide further information about the school and its accomplishments. We are conscious of the special demands of the principal and staff at this time of the year and have organized the task so that compilation will be relatively straightforward and can be shared among several people.

How was this Profile Prepared

1. *Please describe the process by which the profile was prepared.*

The School: Its History and Community

2. *What is the current enrolment in the school?*

3. *Please describe recent and projected enrolment trends.*

4. *Please describe the school community. You may wish to refer to socio-economic status, background and educational interests of parents, local business and industry, historical highlights.*

5. *Please list past events and achievements which have given the school its special nature (this does not call for historical research; we seek reference to those things about the past which are generally known in the school community).*

6. *Briefly describe the major changes which have taken place in the school over about the last five years (included here are educational changes but also changes to staff, buildings, characteristics of the student population and characteristics of the school community).*

7. *What noteworthy changes are anticipated in the next three years (as for Question 6, include here reference to educational changes as well as changes to staff, buildings, characteristics of the student population and characteristics of the school community).*

The Accomplishment(s) for which the School was Nominated

8.   *Please describe the accomplishment(s) in as much detail as space allows.*

9.   *Please give an explanation of how these accomplishments were brought about. Make reference as appropriate to particular people, processes, events or other factors which you believe had an impact.*

10.   *Describe in general terms how leadership is exercised in the school. Distinguish between the role of the principal and that of other school leaders in the school. Consider informal as well as formal leaders.*

11.   *List and briefly describe the roles of the major decision making groups in the school. Include reference as appropriate to groups which include students, parents and other members of the school community.*

Appendix 2:   Interview Questions

Structural

How is the school organized to allow shared decision-making and shared responsibility?

What is it that you and other leaders actively do to promote these arrangements?

How does this contribute to your school's success – for instance, in terms of more effective planning and coordination, or, clearer descriptions of roles?

Other?

Human Resource

In what ways do staff and others support and cooperate with each other – in their teaching practice, or, personally?

What do you and other leaders do to foster such cooperation and support – formally and informally?

How has this influenced school successes, say, in professional development, or, curriculum innovation?

Other?

Political

In what ways is power shared in the school?

What are the preferred processes you and other leaders would engage to ensure consensus is reached – with regard to curriculum decisions or conflict resolution? What processes would you not engage in?

How has this fostered improvement in school outcomes – for example in staff cohesion, or, student and teacher morale?

Other?

Symbolic

What *shared* values run through the daily activities of school life?

What do you and other leaders do to preserve and promote those values – say, in traditions and symbols of the school or informally?

How has this brought about the successes achieved in the school – say, in terms of developing a sense of community or having the collective confidence to manage the challenges faced by urban schools?

Index

accessibility, 111
administration, 41, 43, 51, 108
    culture, 86, 129
    human resource frame, 63
    political frame, 75–6
adult culture, 128
affiliations, 77
alienation, 16, 59
analysis of data, 30–5, 39
Annual General Meetings (AGM), 47–8, 91
anthropology, 15, 134
artistry, 125, 132
assemblies, 91
attitudes, 64, 78, 85, 86, 88
    beliefs, 134
    change, 131, 133
    symbolic frame, 90, 97, 114–15
Australian Principals Associations
    Professional Development Council, 21–2
authoritarianism, 44
autocracy, 129

balkanization, 124, 131
bargaining, 72, 76
Barth, R., 45, 49, 64, 65
Bates, R., 86, 124
Beare, H., 7, 53
Begley, P.T., 27, 70
behaviour, 85, 86, 92
    norms, 101, 114, 116–17
    political, 111
    respect, 93
    students, 102, 110, 119
    vision, 131
behaviourism, 8

beliefs, 85, 86, 87, 88, 123
    change, 131
    collaboration, 134–5
    curriculum, 100
    respect, 93
    symbolic frame, 90, 92, 97
    value-systems, 101
    vision, 131
Bennis, W., 7, 9–10
bias, 36
Bolman, L.G., 13–18, 21, 23, 25
    conceptual issues, 38
    human resource frame, 60, 67
    hypothetical causal links, 99
    political frame, 71, 72, 81
    practice, 130
    reflections, 121–2
    success, 126, 127
    symbolic frame, 85
Burns, J.M., 7, 8, 12

cabals, 39
Caldwell, B.J., 7, 15, 36, 53
caring, 94, 95, 114, 116
causal connections, 99–120
cellular organization, 19–20
centralization, 133
ceremonies see rituals
change, 131, 133
change theory, 8
Cheng, Y.C., 21
choice, 52, 95, 100
Clark, D.L., 59, 125
class size, 51
classroom collaboration, 128–30
cliques, 77
coalitions, 77, 80, 123

collaboration
  beliefs, 134–5
  classrooms, 128–30
  empowerment, 127–8
  rarity, 130–5
collaborative culture, 86, 92, 125, 128
collaborative leadership, 19–27, 118–20
  conceptual framework, 23–5
  definitions, 13–18, 25–7
  political frame, 79–80
  structural frame, 103
  success, 50–3
  symbolic frame, 92–5
collectivism, 134
collegiality, 22, 61, 64, 90, 124
commitment, 89, 92, 131
  democracy, 105
  leadership density, 102
  social justice, 93
  students, 95
communal institutionalizing of vision
    model, 10
community *see also* whole school
    community, 91
computer technology, 129–30
conceptual issues, 38–40
concerts, 48
conflict diffusion, 90
conformity, 134
consensus, 72, 73–4, 76, 79, 80
consultation, 80
contemporary school leadership,
    10–13
contingency views, 8
contingent reward, 11
controls, 41
Cooper, M., 62
cooperation, 59, 60, 62–3, 65, 78
  democracy, 92, 103, 108, 125
  teachers, 100, 109
courage, 90
Cousins, J.B., 27
cultural anthropology, 15, 134
culture, 12, 16, 17–18
  adult, 128
  collaborative, 19, 55–6
  conceptual issues, 39
  definition, 121

diversity, 96, 115
food, 91
forces, 9
human resource frame, 58
power-sharing, 74
social justice, 93
structural frame, 48
student-based, 106
teachers, 65–6
technical, 60–1, 108, 119, 125
curriculum
  beliefs, 100
  change, 79
  choice, 95, 100
  classrooms, 129
  individuality, 102
  innovation, 59, 93, 106–7, 124
  planning, 66
  policy, 46, 81
  students, 101
  success, 94
  symbolic frame, 91

data collection, 30–5, 53–5
Deal, T.E., 13–18, 21, 23, 25, 77, 91
  conceptual issues, 38
  human resource frame, 60, 67
  hypothetical causal links, 99
  political frame, 71, 72, 81
  practice, 130
  reflections, 121–2
  success, 126, 127
  symbolic frame, 85
decentralization, 133
decision-making, 16, 25, 41
  democracy, 29, 55, 79–80, 100, 105
  fair, 111
  individual, 12–13
  negotiation, 82
  parents, 46–7
  participation, 50, 52, 64, 90, 123,
    129
  political frame, 75
  shared, 42
  staff meetings, 43
  teachers, 102–3
  voting, 76
decoding, 18

democracy, 42, 43–4, 45
  decision-making, 55, 79–80, 100
  density of leadership, 122
  empowerment, 133
  meeting procedures, 103–4
  new school, 125
  openness, 104–5
  political frame, 73
  representation, 110
  social justice, 50
  structural frame, 46
  symbolic frame, 89
  teachers, 111–13
democracy, decision-making, 29
density of leadership, 12, 42–3, 49, 102,
    125
  democracy, 122
  empowerment, 132
development of findings, 53–5, 67–8,
    81–3, 95
devil's advocate, 134
directives, 42
disadvantaged children, 87–8, 92, 96,
    113, 115–16, 131–2
discipline, 129
display of data, 31, 34–5
disruption, 111, 123
diversity, 52, 79, 93–4, 114–15, 134
documentation, 91
Drucker, P., 132

educational force, 9
educational potential, 118–19
egalitarianism, 91, 93, 117
electronic mail, 130
empowerment, 8–10, 132–4
  collaboration, 26, 127–8
  culture, 22
  human resource frame, 58
  leadership density, 12
  political frame, 79
  school selection, 29
  structural frame, 44
  students, 100, 102
  symbolic frame, 95
  teachers, 21, 49
  veto, 74
epistemology, 134–5

ethnic teacher aides, 47–8
ethnicity, 87–8, 91
ethos, 17–18, 86

fairness culture, 78
fearlessness, 90
feelings, 58
festivals, 92
findings, 53–6, 67–70, 81–3, 95–7
Firestone, W.A., 124
food, 47–8, 91
forecasting, 99
formal meeting procedures, 45
frame theory, 13, 14–15, 38
free market approach, 52
friendships, 64
Fulghum, R., 136
Fullan, M.G., 9, 21, 22–3, 38
  empowerment, 133–4
  human resource frame, 60, 62, 63, 64
  isolation, 124
  symbolic frame, 90

gender, 8
Giddens, A., 78
Goffman, E., 14
good practice, 39, 130–5
Goodlad, J.I., 20
government reform, 41
Greenfield, T.B., 7
Gronn, P., 11–12

Handy, C., 127
Hargreaves, A., 21, 22–3, 38
  human resource frame, 62, 63
  isolation, 124
  success, 126–7
  symbolic frame, 90
  vision, 131–2
Hocking, H., 36
Holly, P., 126
Huberman, A.M., 31, 36–8, 53, 67, 81
human force, 9
human resource frame, 13–17, 19, 49,
    58–70
  collaborative leadership, 24–6
  conceptual issues, 38
  cooperation, 92

data collection, 32
  hypothesized causal links, 99, 106–9
  individuality, 90
  reflections, 121–2
  success, 126
hypothesized causal links, 99–101, 124
  human resource frame, 106–9
  political frame, 110–13
  structural frame, 102–6
hypothesized causal links, symbolic
  frame, 113–17

ideology, 91
immaturity, 93
improvement, 22, 29–30, 72, 128
individual leadership, 11–12
individualism, 134
individuality, 88–90, 99, 101–2, 115
informal networks, 76–7
information
  availability, 78, 82
  flow, 104–5, 111–12
Inner Melbourne Leadership Project, 23
Inner Melbourne Support Centre, 28, 29,
  78
innovation
  curriculum, 59, 93, 102, 106–7, 124
  improvement, 79, 128
interactive model, 31, 53
interdependence, 59
interest groups, 77
International Congress for School
  Effectiveness and Improvement,
  11
Internet, 130
interviews, 33–4, 37, 39–40
  development of findings, 53–5
  human resource frame, 58–9, 67–8
  political frame, 71–2, 81–3
  structural frame, 42
  symbolic frame, 95–7
isolation, 20, 124, 131
issues, 121–36

Jantzi, D., 22, 38, 61
job opportunities, 88
job satisfaction, 112
Johnson, S.M., 21, 48, 92–3, 121–2, 124
justice, 50, 89, 93

Kanter, R.M., 73
Kennedy, A., 18, 91
King, M.L., 132
Kotter, J.P., 59, 60

language, 33, 39, 91
language styles, 47
leadership *see also* collaborative
  leadership
  collaborative, 19–27
  definitions, 7, 10–11
  human resource frame, 59–65
  political frame, 72–8
  structural frame, 42–50
  symbolic frame, 87–92
  theory, 7–18
learning-enriched schools, 20
Leithwood, K., 11–12, 17, 22, 27, 38, 61,
  70
listening, 25, 26, 42, 73–4
Little, J.W., 20, 45, 60, 61, 124
lobbying, 111
Lortie, D., 19–20
Louis, K., 9
lunchtimes, 91

mainstream thinking, 134
maintenance, 128
management, 108
meanings *see* shared meanings
meeting procedures, 103–4
Meloy, J.M., 59, 125
methodology, research, 28–40
Miles, M.B., 9, 22, 31, 36–8, 53, 67, 81
Millikan, R.H., 7, 53
Ministry of Education, 42, 46, 62, 72,
  78
minute-taking, 45, 55
mixed ability groups, 61, 68
moral beliefs, 134–5
morale, 65, 72, 94, 100
  human resource frame, 58, 106,
  107–8
  political frame, 73
  teachers, 80, 103–4, 109, 115
Morris, L.L., 35
motivation, 62
multi-media, 130

multicultural issues
  festivals, 92
  teacher aides, 29, 48, 78, 82
  teaching, 91

Nanus, B., 7, 9–10
naturalistic methodology, 35
needs, 22, 50, 58, 88, 89
  political frame, 79
  students, 101, 102
  symbolic frame, 94–5
negotiation, 72, 74, 76, 80, 82
networking, 76–8, 100, 123
new school structure, 125
newsletters, 81–2
Nias, J., 20, 38–9, 63, 85–6, 88, 134
norms, 85–7, 92, 134
  behaviour, 101, 114, 116–17
  symbolic frame, 97
  vision, 131

one-sided solutions, 134
open-door policy, 55, 82
organizations
  charts, 15
  healthy, 119–20
  social psychology, 15
  success, 99, 102–6, 106–9, 110–13,
    113–17
  vision, 132

paradox, 126–7, 131
parents, 46–7, 82, 92
participation, 26, 43, 46, 90, 123, 129
  community, 91
  decision-making, 50, 52, 64, 79–80,
    82
  political frame, 73
  power sharing, 110
  responsibility, 55
pastoral care groups, 66
pedagogy, 134–5
personal bias, 36
personal development, 29–30
perspectives *see* frame theory
Peters, T.J., 66
Peterson, K.D., 17–18, 77
philosophy, 106, 123

planning, 15–16, 41, 42, 55
  curriculum, 66
  human resource frame, 63
  team, 108
policy statements, 37–8
policy-making, 15–16
political frame, 14, 15, 17, 19, 71–84
  collaborative leadership, 24, 25, 26
  conceptual issues, 38
  conflict diffusion, 90
  data collection, 32
  hypothesized causal links, 99, 110–13
  reflections, 121–2
  success, 126
political networks, 100–1
political science, 15, 134
postmodernism, 131
power relations, 15, 17, 44, 72, 100
  collaboration, 127–8
  political frame, 72–4, 78
  subcultures, 129
power sharing, 110
prejudices *see also* bias, 58
principal-teacher relationships, 21, 65
problem-solving, 60–1
professional development, 119
psychology, 134
Purkey, S.C., 53

qualitative approach, 30–1, 35–6, 37–8
questionnaires, 32–3, 37–8

rational bonds, 121
reciprocity, 61
reculturing, 131
reduction of data, 31, 34, 38
reflections, 121–36
reform, 41
reframing, 15
relationships, 58, 100, 115, 119, 128–30
reliability of data, 35–7
representation, 110
research, 7–18, 28–40
respect, 26, 43, 93
  change, 131
  diversity, 122
  ethnicity, 91
  political frame, 73–4

power sharing, 110
  symbolic frame, 114, 116
  teachers, 51, 107, 109
responsibility, 42, 43, 45
  individuality, 99
  parents, 46
  participation, 55
  shared, 67, 79
  structural frame, 49
  teachers, 104
rituals, 18, 27, 85
  importance, 87, 92
  symbolic frame, 91, 97
Robbins, S.P., 17, 78
role description, 42
Rosenholtz, S., 20, 38, 60
round table arrangements, 47

Sarros, J.C., 134–5
Schein, E.H., 121–2
school councils, 41–2, 46, 47, 48, 91
  parents, 82
  structural frame, 52
  veto, 74
school-based management, 53
schools
  collaboration background, 19–23
  culture, 85–6
  leadership, 10–13
  new school, 125
  profile, 31, 33, 38, 50–1, 79, 95
  research methodology, 28–30
  success, 50–3
Schools Council, Australia, 90
self-development, 51
self-expression, 100
self-interest, 45–6, 61
self-management, 41
self-worth, 101
Sergiovanni, T.J., 7, 8, 9, 10, 16, 27, 58
  leadership density, 43
  political frame, 73
  reflections, 121–2
  structural frame, 41
  symbolic frame, 17
shared decision-making, 42
shared meanings, 85, 86, 87
shared responsibility, 67, 79
Smith, M.S., 53

social anthropology, 15, 134
social beliefs, 134–5
social events, 63
social justice, 50, 89, 93
social psychology, 134
sociology, 15, 134
Southworth, G., 20, 38, 39, 126
space-use, 91
special needs, 51
Spinks, J.M., 15
staff *see* teachers
staff meetings, 43, 51, 76, 91, 93, 102
Starratt, R.J., 10, 18, 27, 90, 126
Stogdill, R.M., 7
streaming, 101
structural frame, 13, 15–16, 19, 41–57
  collaborative leadership, 23–4, 25, 26
  conceptual issues, 38
  data collection, 32
  decision-making, 90
  hypothesized causal links, 99, 102–6
  meetings, 61–2
  power relations, 77
  reflections, 121–2
  success, 126
student representative councils, 91
student-centred culture, 61–2
students
  commitment, 95
  culture, 128–30
  educational potential, 118–19
  needs, 101
  respect, 93–4
  success, 99–100, 102–9, 110–17, 124
Students at Risk project, 78
study limitations, 37
subcultures, 124, 129
subject choice, 52
subjectivity, 36
success, 50–3, 56, 62, 133
  collaboration, 122–7
  daily practice, 99
  human resource frame, 59, 65–7, 106–9
  political frame, 79–80, 110–13
  structural frame, 102–6
  symbolic frame, 86, 92–5, 113–17

support mechanisms, 59, 62–3, 65, 92, 125
  dismantling, 90
  human resource frame, 67–8
  social welfare, 113
  symbolic frame, 88, 116
  teachers, 107–8
support mechanisms, students, 100
symbolic force, 9–10
symbolic frame, 14, 15, 17–18, 19, 85–98
  collaborative leadership, 24–5, 26–7
  conceptual issues, 38–9
  data collection, 32–3
  empowerment, 134
  hypothesized causal links, 99, 113–17
  reflections, 121–2
  success, 126

Taylor, F., 8
teachers
  collaboration, 19–21
  cooperation, 100
  culture, 65–6, 128–30
  empowerment, 49
  enthusiasm, 106
  human resource frame, 60–1
  isolation, 124
  morale, 80, 94
  professional development, 119
  respect, 51, 93
  social events, 63
  success, 62, 99, 100, 102–9, 110–17, 124–5
  symbolic frame, 88, 92
team effort, 80
team planning, 108
team work, 128
technical culture, 60–1, 108, 119, 125
technical force, 9, 16, 41
technology, 129–30
tertiary education, 88

theologies, 15
theory, 7–18, 125, 130, 134
tracking, 101
traditional culture, 19, 75
traditional teaching methods, 51
transactional leadership, 8, 11–13
transformational leadership, 11–13, 23
transforming leadership, 8

urban schools, 19, 28–30
  collaborative culture, 55–6
  conceptual issues, 39
  human resource frame, 58, 60, 69
  parents, 47–8
  political frame, 83

validity of data, 35–7
value systems, 18, 26–7, 32, 86–7, 123, 134
  beliefs, 101
  respect, 93
  symbolic frame, 85, 90, 97, 114–15
  vision, 131
veto, 44, 74
vision, 9–10, 25, 26, 42, 131–2
  human resource frame, 60
  institutionalization, 120, 125
  political frame, 80
  structural frame, 104, 105
  symbolic frame, 116–17
visits, 37
voting, 73–4, 76

Waterman, R.H., 66
Watkins, P., 74, 75
welfare, 88, 89, 113, 114
whole school community, 88, 94
Wilson, B.L., 124
workgroups, 13, 128

Yeomans, R., 20, 38, 39
Yukl, G., 10